*A BRIEFE HISTORIE OF THE GLORIOUS
MARTYRDOM OF TWELVE
REVEREND PRIESTS*

Father EDMUND CAMPION
& HIS COMPANIONS

By WILLIAM CARDINAL ALLEN

*With Contemporary Verses by the Venerable Henry Walpole,
& the Earliest Engravings of the
Martyrdom*

Reprinted from the (probably unique) Copy in the
British Museum, and edited by the
Rev. J. H. Pollen, S.J.

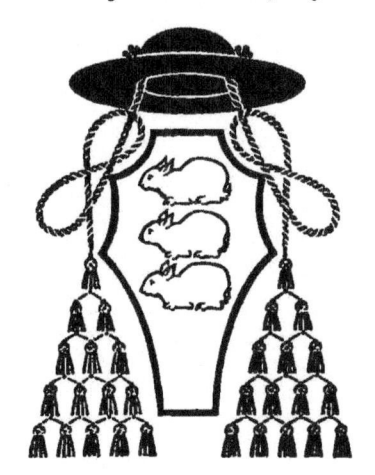

Defecit caro mea et cor meum: Deus cordis mei et pars mea Deus in æternum.—*Psalm* lxxij.
B. EDMUND CAMPION of the Society of Jesus was martyred at London in the year M·DLXXXI

See p. 122

THE INTRODUCTION

THE only explanation, which it is perhaps fitting to make, in introducing this interesting and classical work to the public, would concern the length of time it has been permitted to lie unknown. Every copy but one, so far as I know, has perished, and that copy lies as it were lost, neither referred to by historians, nor mentioned by bibliographers under its distinguished author's name. The explanation is that it originally did its work so well, that it would never have been wholly unknown, and that in altered forms it is popular enough. It has been translated into Latin and Spanish, and twice into Italian; it has also been abbreviated, remodelled and modernized. Its substance is therefore very well known, for this little book is in effect the germ of all the martyrologies that have been written about the sufferers under Queen Elizabeth. A long chapter of bibliography would be needed to set forth all the variously modified forms under which the contents of this book have reached us. I shall return to this subject later, but first a few words about the author.

2. Of William Cardinal Allen, it would be hard indeed to speak too highly. If we except Blessed Edmund Campion, there was perhaps no one among the English Catholics of his day who can be placed higher. Amid all the miseries and sufferings of persecution and exile his co-religionists

greeted him as "our Moses," "Pater Patriæ," "the man upon whom all depends," though it was he who most of all insisted on their enduring those miseries without flinching. The explanation is given us by Campion's words below, p. 26, "Neither shall this Church here ever faile, so long as Priests and Pastors be found for the sheepe; rage man or devil never so much." It was, indeed, due to Campion that this assurance could be given, for it was his glorious zeal which enkindled the spirit of martyrs throughout the whole Catholic community; but it was not only due to Allen that "Priests and Pastors" were actually "found for the sheepe," but he had also been the first to foresee the way out of the difficulty. He had done so at the very moment when the fortunes of Catholicism seemed desperate, and he had devoted life, fortune, influence, everything to the building up of that seminary at Douay in which the "Priests and Pastors" were taught and ordained.

3. Of Allen's power as a writer the little book that follows is a sufficient witness. Not, indeed, that it contains passages of sustained rhetoric, or ingenious argument; on the contrary, no one could carry further "the art of concealing art." The writer has but one object, to set before us the death-scene, as viewed by eyewitnesses, "such as were much conversant with them in their life and present at their arraingement and death." He gives their words as far as he can, reproducing even their use of the first person singular (see note 2). Edmund Bolton, the seventeenth-century critic, considered Allen's *Apologie* "a princely, grave and flourishing piece of exquisite natural English."[1] This praise from the mouth of a Protestant is enhanced by the danger of the times, so that he did not dare declare the opinion to be

[1] See p. xxj

THE INTRODUCTION

his own, but it is "said to be" so. In the same way "many have commended" Father Persons', and "never must be forgotten those .... serious poems, etc, etc., *said to be* father Southwell's." Had Bolton read or been able to speak freely of the volume before us, he would assuredly have commended it more highly still.

4. The following extracts from Allen's letters to Father Agazario of July 7 and September 3, 1582, give the history of the composition of the volume.

"About our brothers and yours, who have lately been murdered, I have already written to you; and deeply grieved though I am, I am now constrained to compose the history of their deaths and of the others. It must be written in English first, for our people desire this very much and send me information for it. Afterwards we shall perhaps also publish it in Latin.

"You will see in it a constancy quite equal to that of the ancient martyrs. Their fortitude has marvellously moved and changed all hearts. Men of good will and moderation are repentant, the wicked and the enemies are amazed. Loud, indeed, is the cry of sacred blood so copiously shed. Ten thousand sermons would not have published our apostolic faith and religion so winningly as the fragrance of these victims, most sweet both to God and to men. The other prisoners have become more courageous, our men are more ready, the harvest increases. With labour and constancy, and God as our leader, we shall conquer. The enemy rages more than ever, for they are desperate.

"Fresh matter for my book is constantly being sent to me. The labour of it, however, all but kills me, for my strength is hardly equal to taking care of the college and of the interests of my countrymen. Now that Bristow and

Martin, by death and sickness, are unable to aid me, my resources are more limited than ever, for there are hardly any others who can help in this sort of work. Still I go on as best I can."

On September 3, 1582, he writes: "I now send you the complete book about the Martyrs. The sheets you have already had as they were printed. We all wish that one of your college or of your society would translate it into Latin. We have no one here with a good style, and are all full of work of this sort. I must at once address myself to a new subject. Our people need intellectual nourishment of this sort, and leave me no rest. Father Robert Persons, the only person who can help me in these matters, is now otherwise and even better occupied."

Next year, August, 1583, he writes explaining why he is slow to continue his work on the martyrs, and why so much has to be passed over in silence. "We have a difficulty in publishing all that we have written. Grave dangers ensue to the Catholics from any detailed description of their persons or affairs. Their names, rank, and holy deeds should indeed be published, and might be read both with pleasure and profit. But the Catholics will not allow it, lest they be betrayed by these indications, and hurried off to prison or even to death. They would be forced to declare who favoured priests, who were their hosts, who helped them through dangers, how they managed to say Mass daily in all the prisons, whence they obtained the vestments necessary for the divine service, how their books and letters and gifts were transferred hither and thither in spite of the constant efforts of their spies and watchmen. There are other things of the same kind more detailed and more wonderful which it would not be right to betray by writing. As soon as ever

THE INTRODUCTION

such things are published, much sooner than anyone would believe, they come to the notice of our enemies."[2]

[2] See p. xxj

5. Father Agazario does not seem to have succeeded in finding a scholar in Rome, as Allen had requested, to translate the book into Latin; he did, however, find some one to translate it into Italian, and it appeared next year, 1583, at Macerata, "appresso Sebastiano Martellini, tradotta di lingua Inglese in Italiana da uno del Collegio Inglese di Roma."[3] The title was *Historia del glorioso martirio di Sedici Sacerdoti, martirisati per la confessione & difesa della fede Catholica*. This edition contains the pictures reproduced at the end of this volume, and there were three or four subsequent editions, some at Macerata and some at Milan.

[3] Ibid.

Meantime the Latin version was not abandoned. It was undertaken, so Father Persons tells us, by Father John Gibbons, S.J., and was published in September, 1583, at Treves, as the *Concertatio Ecclesiæ Anglicanæ* (subsequent editions in 1588 and 1594). From the Latin it was retranslated into Italian in 1595 by Fra Girolamo Pollini, of the Friars Preachers, and into Spanish in 1599 by Fray Diego Yepez, Bishop of Tarragona, each of them doing something to enlarge the book and bring it up to date. By this time, therefore, Allen's tract had swelled out by accretions to three or four times its original bulk. In the seventeenth century the tendency was to condense, and instead of "Lives," we get the long series of *Catalogues of the Martyrs*.[4] The lists of authorities cited by these catalogues show that Cardinal Allen's work had by now been forgotten, its place having been taken by the bulkier translations mentioned above. Dr Challoner knew the book, though he did not know who was the author, and has quoted from it in many places. After this it falls altogether out of sight. Until the publi-

[4] Ibid.

cation of Cardinal Allen's letters, no one knew he had written it. It was not ascribed to him by Simpson or Gillow, or the British Museum Catalogue, where it was practically buried under the heading, "Catholic Faith."

From all this one can see how it came about that, though the message of the volume has not only not been lost, but gradually become more and more familiar and popular, the author's own words have vanished from view or been weakened by later changes.

6. If any wish to read the stories of the martyrs with special thoroughness, they may be commended the comparative method. Our martyrs suffered, as a rule, under the same laws and procedure, and they had also been through similar courses of education, and lived the lives which were fairly like one another. Hence it is that their "Acts" do really enlighten one another. The first point of similarity we shall note is that though the first four martyrs were representative of the whole Catholic body, namely, a layman, a secular priest, one member of Oxford University, and another of Cambridge, yet the following nine were all Oxonians. It was long before the Old Faith could be completely uprooted at that University, and the fellows, as they were ejected, often went over to the Douay Seminary. Three out of the thirteen had received Anglican Orders, and it is instructive to note what was thought of those rites at that early period (pp. 6, 98, 108). We also find evidences of the prevalence of "going to Protestant Churches," that sin which was the chief cause of the great loss of faith during the early part of Elizabeth's reign, though afterwards valiantly resisted (pp. 40, 96, 117). Of the missionary life Allen, for reasons already given by him, says little or nothing.

The arrest of the martyrs might take place in many ways.

THE INTRODUCTION

Generally the house in which they were living was betrayed and searched. At that early period of the persecution there were but few hiding-places. Campion and Ford were found in one (p. 10), though not without great difficulty; Sherwin and Mayne were in their rooms (pp. 39, 105); Briant was seized at midnight in bed (p. 48); Filby was taken by watchmen (p. 11); Sherwood was cried upon in the streets (p. 118); when seized they were searched "unto their skinnes" (p. 84); and they were generally relieved of their spare cash, "a principal verb in the apprehension of all Catholics" (pp. 48, 89), and a very grievous hardship, when prisoners had to pay their own expenses. They were then dragged to prison, often amid insults (pp. 10, 105, and plates 1, 2). In prison they were burdened with chains, "great bolts," "gyves" or "shackles" (pp. 11, 12, 20, 39, 50), which were sometimes so heavy and galling that one hand had to be used to hold them up (p. 101). Sometimes they had much to suffer from hunger and thirst (pp. 48, 49, 119), and want of bedding (pp. 50, 76). But the servants of God frequently mortified themselves by voluntary fasting, disciplines and rough hair shirts (pp. 34, 40, 83) to prepare for the greater combat still before them. For prudential reasons already mentioned, Allen says nothing of the opportunities of saying Mass, etc., which the martyrs might enjoy by connivance of keepers. But the case of Nelson (p. 113) had taken place four years before, and it could therefore be quoted with little danger. The affection of the martyrs for small practices and objects of devotion, especially the cross, is everywhere apparent (sign of the cross, pp. 57, 62, 67; small wooden cross, pp. 50, 68; cross in Cheapeside, p. 12; Agnus Dei and holy grains, i.e., beads, p. 105).

At one time or other nearly all the martyrs had to defend

their Faith by *disputation*. Indeed, they often looked forward to this with almost too much joy and confidence (pp. 9, 15, 24, 27, 39, 40). The debate was sometimes "pretie and plesant" (p. 11), but when the Catholics began "to grip their adversaries hard, they parted them with their tipstaves" (a metaphor from bear-baiting, p. 15), or avoided the engagement altogether (p. 39). A more serious matter was the examination as to their hosts (p. 39), their converts (p. 13), and even what may be called confessional secrets (p. 88). To extract information on these heads the torture of the rack was freely used (pp. 3, 12-14, 17, 19, 27, 30, 32, 39, 59, 60, 80, 88, 96, 119; inability to move the hands after racking, pp. 17, 96). Though forbidden by English law, the Tudor tyrants regarded torture as one of their prerogatives, to be exercised, however, only in the Tower, and by special warrant. In one case we hear of needles being thrust under the nails (p. 49). This was unusual, and may be connected with the procedure for witch-finding. The poor sufferer in this case was one who at one time fell into a sort of trance, during which he was "without sense and feeling well nigh of all grief and pain," which he himself thought might be miraculous (p. 53). On another occasion we hear of a martyr being, by way of indignity, indicted in company with witches (p. 89).

Little attempt is made to describe the trials (pp. 16-20, 89, 106), and the dreadful sentence is said to be "well-known to all men" (p. 101). After condemnation, they were, according to the barbarous custom of the day, cast into the low Walesboure dungeon in the Tower (p. 50), and the "low dungeon" (otherwise called the "pit" or "limbo") at Newgate (p. 114), or at least "yrons were commanded upon them, as soon as they came home, and never taken

THE INTRODUCTION

off till they were fetched forth to be martyred" (pp. 20, 50). This summons was generally given early in the morning (pp. 57, 67), and if in the Tower (where most of this band of sufferers were confined) they were assembled in Coldharbour (p. 20), an open spot on the south-west of the White Tower, where there is now a collection of ancient cannon. The hurdle (car or sled) was large enough to carry two victims (p. 1), who were tied down to it and so "trailed" or "drawn" along the ground (pp. 1, 57, 62, 67, 88, 93, 115). In ancient times the condemned had been literally dragged at the horse's tail, and this may explain the otherwise extraordinary suggestion made about Mayne (p. 107). According to sentence they were dragged "through the middle of the city," so, though the route is not specified, we may be pretty sure that it ran by Tower Street, Cheapside, Newgate, Snow Hill, High Holborn, St Giles's, Oxford Street, to Tyburn in the fork of the Edgware and Bayswater Roads. A new gallows had been erected there for the execution of Blessed John Storey (1572), and it had now the name of "Gallows of the Martyrs" (p. 21). Though they were "by the way molested by ministers for their subversion" (p. 1 and plate 5), it was often possible during the long route for comforters to draw near, and a gentleman "courteously wiped off Campion's face the mire wherewith he was all to bemoyled" (note 1).

Upon arrival at the place of execution, a proclamation for keeping the peace was read (p. 68). The martyrs were not immediately let free from the hurdle, but while the first was hanging the second was brought up and made to "turn backward" and look at the first, while he was quartered (pp. 74, 77, 78, 81). Occasionally, under more favourable circumstances, they were allowed to kneel and pray (pp. 93, 107), but generally the time for devotion was short, as the officials and the "vulgar pulpit-men" (p. 8) left them little peace. Standing in the cart, and having the rope round their necks, they generally began their last prayers with the sign of the cross (pp. 62, 67, 77, 110, cf. 12), and the *Pater*, *Ave* and *Credo* in Latin. Sooner or later they would be called upon to pray in English or with the Protestants. The latter was uniformly refused (pp. 4, 66, 69, 74, 83, 102, 115).

Then came, under one form or another, what the Catholics were wont to call "the bloody question," namely, what did they think of the excommunication of the Queen by Pope Pius V? (pp. 4, 16, 35, 47, 58, 68, 72, 100, 101, 118.) It should be explained that the martyrs were not condemned to death for this matter, but certain alleged acts of treason, "practising the Queen's deposition and death, stirring rebellion and invasion of the Realm" (p. 17), and it was for this that they were to be executed. There was no statute that made it treason to have *an opinion* on the validity of the Pope's sentence (*pace* Sheriff Martin, p. 64), as Kirby and Johnson told Topcliffe and others (pp. 72, 78). Nelson had, indeed, with injustice too glaring to be often repeated, been brought "by course of questions" about the Bull "into the compass of the new statutes of treason." But then he had not warded off with sufficient cleverness the insinuation that he gave his opinion "in order to persuade others to be of his mind" (pp. 99-101). On the present occasion the "bloody question" could only have been put *ad captandum vulgus*. It was inevitable that the opinion of a Catholic, however moderate (pp. 58, 68, 70, 72), on this point should seem unsatisfactory to the fanatics, who came to gloat over the slaughter of the priests. They would be

THE INTRODUCTION

excited against the martyrs, and the execution could take place without much attention being given to the palpable injustice of the charges actually alleged against them (p. 19, 58, 60). The more ordinary response of the martyrs was that of Father Campion, which was also, on the whole, the most dignified (pp. 4, 16, 35, 47). The clearness and emphasis with which the martyrs acknowledged Elizabeth as their Queen, and prayed for her, is very remarkable indeed (pp. 5, 35, 59, 61, 64, 68, 70, 73, 78, 82, 90, 93 94), so remarkable that the onlookers, unable, alas! through prejudice to believe their own ears, actually inquired "for which Queen he prayed" (pp. 5, 36, 68, 70). The sentiments of their biographers (pp. 28, 46) are also well deserving of note. Some martyrs, with honourable pride, "defied treason" (p. 93), and all refused to ask pardon for their offences (pp. 5, 35, 47, 60, 69, 80, 93, 101), or to acknowledge the Royal Supremacy in matters ecclesiastical (pp. 61, 64, 110, 111). Offers of life were freely made even now if the martyrs would yield (pp. 20, 57, 61, 64, 69, 73, 80, 82).

Eventually the order was given to drive away the cart, when at Tyburn, or to turn the ladder at smaller scaffolds (pp. 95, 107, 108). The last words of the Martyrs at this moment are often given. They are usually from the *Jesus Psalter*, so popular in those days (pp. 36, 59, 95). Otherwise they said the *Ave* (pp. 81, 83), the *Miserere* (p. 48), or *In manus tuas* (pp. 64, 108), or "Lord, receive my soul" (pp. 69, 81, 116). Shert used a beautiful prayer from the *Sarum Horæ* (p. 62), now unhappily forgotten.

In most cases they were cut down when half dead according to sentence. But there were also instances in which they were allowed to hang till they were dead, or quite insensible (pp. 69, 74, 83, 96, 108). To ensure this result "Bull, the hangman of Newgate" (who was sometimes tipped to show that no ill will was felt against him, pp. 61, 79, 96), would "set the knot to the ear," and the bystanders would draw down the sufferer's legs or arms (pp. 62, 69, 96). The head, when cut off, was held up with the cry, "God save the Queen" (pp. 70, 78, 82). It was afterwards generally set on London Bridge and the quarters on the City gates (pp. 30, 33, 116, 119, cf. 108).

7. The Verses. Among the most remarkable results of Campion's death were the numerous pieces of verse which it occasioned. No other of our martyrs evoked the enthusiasm which these lines, when considered in their circumstances, so strikingly manifest. Some shorter pieces are collected by Simpson, *Campion* (p. 268), and a longer composition, *A Brief of the Life and Death of Sir Edmund Campion*, will be found in my *Acts of English Martyrs* (p. 23). The verses here reproduced were printed by Stephen Vallenger in the *True Report of the Death and Martyrdome of M. Campion, Jesuite, whereunto is annexid certayne verses made by sundrie persons.* This is a very rare little booklet, unknown to such careful writers as Dr Jessopp, the only copy with which I am acquainted is that of the British Museum (1370 a. 80, *under* Campion, Edmund). Dr Allen's book may, in a certain way, be regarded as a second edition of the *True Report*, in so far as he faithfully takes over, verbatim, or nearly so, the whole of Vallenger's history, omitting the introductory and apologetic paragraphs (i.e., Allen's, pp. 2-5, correspond with the *True Report* sig. B vij to C ij; pp. 34-36 with sig. C iv to C viij; pp. 47, 48 with sig. D iij, D iv). It is, therefore, clearly appropriate to restore these verses to the history they were originally meant to adorn.

As to their author or authors we have no absolute certainty,

THE INTRODUCTION

but there seems good reason for believing the first to have been by Henry Walpole, himself afterwards a Jesuit martyr. We know from Father Persons (about 1608) that Walpole was connected with the bringing out of the *True Report*, and afterwards had to fly for his life (*Catholic Record Society*, IV, 38). Not long after this, Father Christopher Walpole, S.J., Henry's brother, told Father N. Southwell (Bacon) that the martyr "had written the verses" in the book. I fancy that he did not really write them all, for they seem by their style to be by different hands, while if one person had set himself to compose four sets of verses on the subject, he would probably have divided up his subject with some care, but would occasionally have lapsed into similar expressions; whereas these pieces treat the same topics but with different phraseology and ideas. Then, too, Father Christopher Grene, a somewhat later but very careful writer, has stated that Walpole is "reported to be the writer of the first and of the second poem" (Stonyhurst MS. *Collectanea* N i, 3). Finally, we have the analogy of the translation of St Peter Damian's hymn (also erroneously ascribed to St Augustine), *Ad perennis vitæ fontem mens sitivit arida*, "My thirsty soul desyres her draught," with its undersong beginning, "Jerusalem, thy joys divine" (printed in *The Month*, 1871, II, 235). This is also ascribed to Walpole by Grene, and its diction has many points of resemblance to "Why do I use my paper, ink and pen?"

There is a very carefully made manuscript copy of "Why do I use" in the Bodleian Library, the variant readings of which are given in note 8. A still stronger testimony to the popularity of the lines is found in their having been set to music by William Byrd, organist of Elizabeth's Chapel Royal, a man of well-known Catholic tendencies. In his

Medius: Psalmes, Sonets and Songs of Sadnes and Pietie, 1588, he published this hymn, but in an Anglican version. The first verse is preserved, but the following verses are rewritten. The references to Campion are removed, and "The Martirs of ancient times" are praised in his place. Father Morris reprinted the original text of "Why do I use" in *The Month*, 1872, January, p. 118.

7. In editing I have followed the generally approved principle of keeping the original spelling, but supplementing the defective punctuation. It should be noticed that this spelling is that of Allen's (unknown) printer, which is somewhat different from his own, as to which see pp. 86, 132, 315 of his *Letters*. With this in view I have occasionally reverted to Allen's own spelling of "one" and "all" for "on" and "al," which the printer preferred, but which are sometimes rather confusing to us. The breaking into paragraphs is also generally my doing.

The original title page runs as follows:

A | Briefe Historie of the Glorious Martyrdom | of xij Reverend Priests, | executed within these twelve monethes | for confession and defence of the Catholike | Faith. But under the false pretence of Treason | With a note of sundrie things that befel them in | their life and imprisonment: and a preface declaring their innocencie. | Set furth by such as were much conuersant | with them in their life, and present at their arraignement and death. | Occidistis, sed non possedistis | that is | You have slain them, but you have | not gotten possession.

8vo. No place or date. Pp. 158; sig. *a* to *f* in 8s, and *A* to *D* in 8s. The print of the original is very small, the same size as that used here for the notes. I have omitted Campion's Latin letter, on which see note 7, and the Latin

THE INTRODUCTION

verses at p. 92, *Sit mihi fas Edmunde* (reprinted in *Concertatio*, p. 66). Also the long *Introduction*, which, though excellent, is in effect controversy not history, and the examinations of the Martyrs, which have been frequently reprinted elsewhere (e.g., Tierney's Dodd, III, ap. iv). On the other hand I have *inserted* the *verses* from Vallenger's *True Report*, which for reasons stated above have a certain right to a place here, and I have also added the cuts from the first Italian translation of this work (p. 120 below).

J. H. POLLEN, S.J.

[1] *Hypercritica*, ed. Bolton, *N. Triveti Annales*, appendix, p. 233.
[2] F. Knox, *Letters of Cardinal Allen*, pp. 148, 160, 203.
[3] *Catholic Record Society*, III, p. 110. There is a description of the rare first edition, vol. v, p. 143.
[4] *Catholic Record Society*, v, pp. 1-17, contains a list of them, with a partial analysis of their contents.

THE CONTENTS

The Introduction
Chap. I Of F. Campion, Priest of the Societie of
    Jesus   1
  II M. Ralph Sherwine, Priest   34
  III Of M. Alexander Brian, Priest   47
  IV The Martyrdom of M. Thomas Forde, M.
    John Sherte and M. Robert Johnson   57
  V Of Mr John Shert, Priest   59
  VI M. Robert Johnson, Priest   62
  VII The Martyrdom of M. William Filbie   67
  VIII Of M. Luke Kirbie, Priest   69
  IX Of M. Laurence Richardson and M.
    Thomas Cottam   77
  X The Order of the Arraignement and Martyrdom of M. John Paine, Priest   89
  XI The Arraignement and Martyrdom of M.
    Everard Haunse, Priest   98
  XII Of M. Cuthbert Maine, Priest   104
  XIII Of M. John Nelson, Priest   111
  XIV The Martyrdom of Thomas Sherwod   118
The Illustrations   120
The Notes   135
The Index   137

A TRUE REPORT OF THE DEATH
& MARTYRDOM OF F. CAMPION, JESUITE
and Priest, of M. Sherwin and M. Bryan Priestes

Pro veræ virtutis præmiis falsi sceleris pœnas subimus.
For the reward of true virtue we bear the penalties of fictitious crime.
Boetius, lib. i *De Consolatione Philosophiæ.*

AND FIRST OF F. CAMPION PRIEST
of the Societie of the name of Jesus, Bachiler of Divinitie, & some time fellow of S. John Baptist's Colledge in Oxford.

Chap. I

THESE THREE GLORIOUS Confessors, learned, meeke, godly and constant Priests, upon the first day of December in the yere of our Lord 1581, were (under pretence of high treason, most injuriously, to the great lamentation generally of all good men) drawen from the Tower to Tyborne, there to be Martyred for the Catholike Faith and religion. *F. Campion* was alone on one herdle, the other two together on another. All were molested by Ministers and others calling upon them by the way for their subversion; and by some also (as opportunitie served, and as in a case of so great daunger it conveniently might be) comforted, and *F. Campion* specially, by

THE DEATH & MARTYRDOM

one that consulted him in some cases of conscience and religion, and the myre wherewith he was all to bemoyled[1] most courteously wiped off his face.

When they were come to the place of execution, where divers of her Maiestie's honorable Council with many honorable personages and Gentilmen of worship and good accompt, beside an infinit multitude of people, attended their coming, *F. Campion* was first brought up into the carte: where, after some smale pawse, and after the great rumor of so many people somewhat appeased, with grave countenance & sweet voice, he stoutly spake as followeth:

'*Spectaculum facti sumus Deo, Angelis & hominibus*.' Saying, These are the wordes of *S. Paule*, Englished thus: We are made a spectacle, or a sight unto God, unto His Angels, and unto men: verified this day in me; who am here a spectacle unto my Lord God, a spectacle unto His Angels, and unto you men.'

And here going forward in his text, was interrupted and cut off by *Sir Francis Knowles* and the Sherifes, ernestly urging him to confesse his treason against her Maiestie & to acknowledge himself guiltie. To whom he answered saying: 'For the treasons, which have been laid to my charge, and which I am come here to suffer for, I desire you all to beare witnesse with me, that thereof I am altogether innocent.'

Whereupon, answer was made to him by one of the Council, that he might not seeme to deny the objections against him, having been proved so manifestly to his face, both by sufficient witnes and evidence. 'Well, my Lord (quoth *F. Campion*) I am a Catholike man and a Priest; in that faith have I lived hitherto, and in that faith I do entend to dye; and if you esteeme my religion treason, then of

---

See Note 1

See Note 2
Mundo *in the text.*

They would not suffer him to speake on religion lest he should have perswaded the people

force I must graunt³ unto you. As for any other treason, I never committed any; God is my Judge. *See Note 3*

'But you have now what you do desire, I beseech you to have patience, and suffer me to speake a worde or two, for discharge of my conscience.'

But being not suffered to goe forward, he was forced to speake onely to that point which they most urged; protesting that he was guiltless and innocent of all treason and conspiracie, craving credit to be given to his answers, as to a last answere made upon his death and soule. He added that touching this point, both the Jurie might easely be deceived, and more also put into the evidence then was true. Notwithstanding he forgave, as he would be forgiven; desiring all of them to forgeve him whom he had confessed upon the rack (*for upon the commissioners' othes, that no harme should come unto them, he uttered some persons with whom he had been*). *His innocencie* — *A time when such a man would never lye* — *Great charitie*

Further he declared the meaning of a letter sent by himself in time of his imprisonement to *M. Pound*, a captive then also in the Tower, in which he wrot, he would not disclose the secrets of some howses where he had ben entertained, affirming on his soule, that the secrets he meant in that letter were not, as it was misconstred by the ennemie, treason or conspiracie, or any matter els any way entended against her Maiestie or the state; but saying of *Masse*, hearing of *confessions, preaching* and such like dueties and functions of *Priesthod*. This he protested to be true, as he would answer before God. *He expoundeth his letter, falsely construed by the adversaries* — *Which in these miserable daies must be done as secretly as murder or treason*

Then he desired *Sir Francis Knowles*, and some other of nobilitie to heare him touching one *Richardson* condemned about a booke of his, and earnestly besought them to have consideration of that man, saying, he was not that *Richard-*

4 THE DEATH & MARTYRDOM

son which brought his booke, and this he affirmed with vehement protestation upon his death. (*This notwithstanding*, Richardson *was executed, one man for another, quid pro quo like il poticario*⁴).

Then one *Hearne*, a schole maister, as I lerned after, red the new *advertisement* openely with loude voice to the people, published only to coulor so manifest and expresse injustice. F. *Campion* all the time of his reading devoutely praying.

Notwithstanding which *advertisement*⁵ or defence of theirs, as well because they distrusted their own pollicie in publication thereof, as that they did also desire some better coulor or faster visard for their procedings, they pressed him to declare his opinion of *Pius quintus* Bull concerning the excommunication of the Queene. To which demaund he gave no answere.

But being asked whether he renounced the Pope, said he was a *Catholike*. Whereupon one inferred, saying: 'In your Catholicisme (I noted the worde) all treason is conteined.' In fine, preparing himself to drinke his last draught of *Christ's* cup, he was interrupted in his praier by a Minister willing him to say, '*Christ*, have mercie upon me' or some like praier with him. Unto whom he loking backe with milde countenance humbly said: '*You and I are not one in religion. Wherefore I pray you content yourself. I barre none of praier; only I desire them of the household of faith to pray with me, and in my agonie to say one Creede*' (for a signification that he died for the confession of the Catholike faith therein contained).

Some also called on him to pray in English, to whom he answered, that he would pray in a language that he well understood. At the upshot of this conflict he was willed to aske the Queene forgevenes and to pray for her.

Sidenotes:
See Note 4
A new practise to coulor their iniustice
See Note 5

Catholicisme is treason in Atheisme

Catholikes may not pray with Heretikes

And God too

OF FATHER EDMUND CAMPION 5

He meekely answered: '*Wherein have I offended her? In this I am innocent, this is my last speach, in this give me credit, I have and do pray for her.*' Then did the Lord *Charles Howard* aske of him, For which queene he praied, whether for Elizabeth queene, to whom he answered, '*Yea for* Elizabeth *your queene and my queene.*' And the carte being drawen away, he meekly and sweetly yelded his soule unto his Saviour, protesting that he died a perfect Catholike.

Which his mylde death and former sincer protestations and speaches of his innocencie, moved the people to such compassion and teares, that the adversaries in their printed bookes[6] were glad to excuse the matter.

So gratiously and gloriously this blessed man ended and overcame in Christ all these mortal miseries, now enjoying in heaven the triumphant crowne of his happy confession and Martyrdom, made by God's providence before all London, the place of his nativitie: that such of his citizens as were not worthie to enjoy the life and labours of one of the famousest persons that their citie hath bredde in our memorie, may yet, either by his sacred innocent bloude, powred out here amonge them, or by his holy praiers, which he now doubtles maketh, both for his loving frendes and deadly persecutors, be converted from their damnable and palpable errors.

He lived in this worlde about fortie and two yeres. After his childhod and education in London, he was brought up in S. *John's Colledge* of Oxford, passingly beloved for his singular graces, of the founder thereof, *Sir Thomas White* of worthie memorie, at whose burial he made an eloquent oration in Latine, having made the like before in English at the funerals of my *Ladie Dudley*, late wife to the *Ear* of *Leicester*. Where after he had passed with all

Innocencie

In the booke printed in Mundaie's name, of his death

See Note 6

F. Campion martyred by God's providence in the citie of his nativitie

He praieth for his frends and enemies

His age

THE DEATH & MARTYRDOM

He passed through all offices in the universitie

commendation through such exercises, degrees and offices, as the universitie yeldeth to men of his condition: though he were never wholy inclinable to the sectes of this time, yet by the importunate perswasions of some of his frendes, much desirous for his worldly honor and advancement to have him come to the pulpite and take livinges, he suffered himself to be made deacon after their newe manner, not well knowing then howe odible to God that and the rest of their schismatical degrees be.

He went to Irland and wrot the storie thereof eloquently. He went to the Seminarie at Douay. He proceeded Bachiler of divinitie

But for all that our Lord mercifully withheld him from that ambitious course which is the goulfe that many goodly wittes have perished in, in these daies. Therefor spending some more time in study and travailing into Irland, the historie of which countrey he wrotte very truly and eloquently, hearing that there was a Seminary not longe before begonne in Doway, thither he went where after a yere's great diligence and many exercises done booth in house and publike scholes, he proceded bachilier of divinitie, to his great commendation, and the honor of our nation.

His trouble of minde for taking scismatical orders

Nevertheless all this while, specially being now of more devotion, zeale, lerning and iudgement then before, the continual cogitation of that schismatical order of English deaconshipe which he had taken did so sore oppresse his minde, and the conceite of the greatnes of that sinne so burdened his conscience, that no counsel of lerned frendes could geve him satisfaction, nor otherwise deliver him of the fearful conceit of that prophane degree, till he entered into religion, by penance and holy profession to wipe away the same.

He went to Rome and there entered into religion.

So making his choise of the societie of the name of Jesus, he went to Rome, where by the superior of that order he was admitted, and so, not remaining in the citie much more

OF FATHER EDMUND CAMPION

than a moneth, he was sent into Beameland, where he abode viij yeres, and was made Priest in Prage, continually teaching, preaching, catechizing, writing and travailing for the church of God. Whereby he became so famous, that not onely other principal states, but the Imperial Maiestie was contented often to heare him preach. Till at length by the sute of such as knewe his great graces in dealing with heretikes for their conversion, his general called him thence to be bestowed upon his owne native countrey.

Whitherwarde by longe and great travail he came, going about by Rome (because his superiors knewe him not, nor would not send him before they sawe him) and by Remes, where, besides other communication parteining to the reduction of our countrey to the Catholike faith, he demaunded of *D. Allen* whether he thought that any service he could do in England, the time being as it is, were like to be worth all these long labours and hazardes past and to come, or might countervaile the lackes that those should seeme to have by his absence from whence he came. To which *Doctor Allen* answered: 'Father (quoth he) first, whatsoever you did there, may be done by others, one or mo of your order. Secondly, you owe more duetie to England then to Beameland, and to London then to Prage: though it liketh me well that you have made some recompence to that countrey for the old wounde it received by us. Thirdly, the recoverie of one soule from heresie, is worth all your paines, as I hope you shall gaine a great many: because the harvest is both more plentiful and more ripe with us, then in those partes. Finally, the reward may be greater, for you may be martyred for it at home, which you can not obtaine lightely there.' So he was satisfied, and of this communication I have heard him often speake.

He is sent into Beameland & made priest. He preacheth befor the Emperour

He is sent home again by his superiors

His communication with D. Allen

D. Allen's answer

In Wicliffe's time, of whom they lerned their heresies

And at last he happely landed at Dover upon the morrow after Midsomer-day, the yere 1580, being by God's great goodnes delivered out of the searchers' and officers' handes, who held him with them upon suspicion for certaine houres, upon deliberation to have sent him to the Council.

That was Christe's special worke and providence, to be glorified booth in his preaching a whole yere, to the inspeakable good of innumerable deceived soules, and also in his precious death afterward. Comming therefore to London, he preached there his first sermon upon *SS. Peter and Paule's* day, which I was at my selfe, having a full audience and very worshipful. But afterward booth there, and in sundry partes of the realme, far greater, through the fame and experience of his manifold vertues, great eloquence and lerning, many Protestantes of good nature at sundry times admitted also to the same, who ever afterward contemned their vulgar pulpit men in comparison of him.

The first man of calling to whose howse he was conducted in the countrey, demaunded of the person that brought him thither, being himselfe of good worship, what he was and from whence he came. And lerning that he was a religious man, and one that had bene long in foraine partes: before he would admitte him, toke him aside and asked the causes of his retorne home, and repaire to him; and whether he meant not under coulor of religion to withdraw her Maiestie's subiects from their obedience.

To which he answered, protesting befor God, that he had neither other commission of his superiors, nor intention of himself, then to minister the holy Sacraments, preach, and teach the people to salvation; and that he neither could nor would medle with matter of state. Whereupon the par-

The day of his arrival in England

He was taied at Douer

His first sermon

The speaches betwixt him & the gentilman, in whose house he first preached in the countrey

OF FATHER EDMUND CAMPION 9

tie embraced him, and bid him hartely welcome to his howse. Finding afterward by a littel further acquaintance, which all the world might see, that he was no man for worldly matters, but only for the schole, Church and pulpit, wherein his giftes were excellent, in the highest degree.

And from that day, till his apprehension, he preached once a day at the least, often twise and sometimes thrise, whereby through God's goodnes he converted sundry in most shires of the Realme, of most wisdome and worshipe, besides yong Gentilmen studentes and others of all sortes. *He preached daily and often. He converted many of the best sort*

At his first entrance he made his proffer of disputation for such causes as he alleaged in the same, and more at large afterward in his eloquent and lerned booke to both the universities. Whereby the Protestant Preachers and Prelates found themselves so deeply wounded in their doctrine and credite, notwithstanding they had patched up a few pamphletes without all grace against him, that they pricked her Maiestie's Councel to alter the question from controversie in religion to the cause of the Prince and matter of state; that so they might defende that by force and authoritie, which they could not do by all their lerning and divinitie. *His chalendg and his booke written to the universities*

The Protestants devise to overthrow him

Thereupon it was geven out by divers speaches and proclamations, that great confederacies of Pope and foraine Princes were made for the invasion of the Lande, and that the Iesuistes and Seminary Priestes were sent in forsoth to prepare their waies: and such like trumperie, to beguile and incense the simple against them. Then all exquisite diligence was used for the apprehension of others, but specially of *F. Campion*, whom being but one among thousandes of the Churche's children, nor the cheefe in England of his order, yet they called the Pope's Champion and right hand. *The follie of the adversarie*

THE DEATH & MARTYRDOM

Eliot the traitor

His apprehension

And in what sort

His charitie

His patrone

His behaviour

His carrying up to London

At length after he had laboured in God's harvest well nere xiij Monethes, by the notorious wickednes of one *George Eliote* a forelorne fellow, such as for affliction of holy men this world commonly useth, after long search and much a doe, by God's permission he fell into the persecutors' hands the xvij of Iuly 1581, being found in a secret closset in a Catholike Gentilman and confessor's house called *Mr Yates of Lyford*. Twoe godly Priests *M. Forde* and *M. Collington* being with him, all lying, when the ennemy discovered them, upon a bed, their faces and handes lifted up to heaven. He offered his ij fellowes before in the time of the search, that if they thought all that a doe was for him, and that his yelding might acquite them, he would geve himselfe up to their handes. But they would not suffer that in any wise; but hearing one another's confession expected God's good will together, every one having enioyned penance to say thrise, *Fiat Voluntas tua, domine*, 'Thy will be fulfilled,' and *Sancte Joannes Baptista, ora pro me*, 'Saint John Baptist, pray for me.' Which blessed Saint they principally praied unto, for that the said *F. Campion* was delivered, as he toke it, out of the searchers' handes at Dover, by the holy mediation of that holy prophet, his special patrone.

But *F. Campion* the man of God, being now in the power of his said traditor and the officers, and made a spectacle and matter of mockerie to the unwise multitude and ungodly of all sortes, shewed such marckable modestie, myldness, patience and Christian humilitie in all his speaches and doings, that the good were excedingly edified and the ennemies much astonied.

After ij daies that he was in the Sherife of Barkeshire's custodie he was caried with the rest as well Priests as Gentilmen, and other in that place apprehended, towards London. In the way he had many pretie and plesant disputes, speeches & answers with the Gentilmen that garded him, and other that came to see him: to their wonderful liking and admiration of his so cheereful and Christian behaviour, in the middest of his destresses, which to the worldly there about him seemed intolerable, but to him that had such an inward man they were nothing.

At Abington, among others, divers schollers of Oxford came to see the man so famous, whereof being tolde by one *M. Lidcote*, he said he was very glad, himselfe being once of that universitie, and asked whether they would heare a sermon. There at dinner, *Eliote* said unto him, '*M. Campion*, you looke cherefully upon every body but me. I knowe you are angrie with me in your hart for this worke.' 'God forgeve thee, *Eliot* (said he) for so iudging of me. I forgeve thee, and in token thereof I drinke to thee. Yea, and if thou wilt repent and come to confession, I will absolve thee; but large penance thou must have.' *[Eliot's speech to F. Campion]*

Afterward at Henley *M. Filby* a Priest and one of the prisoners (not found in the house with the rest, but taken in the watch, as he was comming to the house) had in his sleepe a significant dreame or vision, of the ripping up of his body and taking out of his bowels: the terrour whereof caused him to cry so loud that the whole house was raised therby, which afterward in his owne, *F. Campion's*, and other his fellowes' Martyrdom was accomplished. *[M. Filbie's strange dreame]*

Besides the tying of their legges under the horses' bellies, and binding their armes behind them, which was done to others also, the Counsel appointed special punishment and disgraces for *F. Campion*, not ever wont to be done till the partie were convicted of some crime, commaund- *[Disgraces donne to F. Campion]* ing a paper to be set upon his hat with great capital letters shewing him to be *Campion the seditious Iesuit*, as the Herodians once revested his Maister for the like cause, and in like kind of mockerie with kingly robe, crowne and scepter.

And to take their further pleasure of him order was geven they should stay at Colbrucke a good piece of Friday and all night, that thence they might bring him and his fellowes upon Saturday in triumph through the citie and the whole length thereof, specially through such places where by reason of the markets of that day, the greatest concourse of the common people was, whom in such matters they seeke of pollicie most to please, which was executed accordingly. All London almost beholding the spectacle, the simple gasing and with delite beholding the noveltie, the wise lamenting to see our country fallen to such barbarous iniquitie as to abuse a sacred man so honorable in all nations for his lerning and of so innocent a life.

When he came by the crosse in Chepe, in the best maner he could (being pinyoned), he Christianly made the signe of our Saviour upon his brest and with like humilitie deeply bent his bodie for reverence towardes Christ's image there, which was a strange sight to the deceived people of that place.

So that day which was the xxij of Iuly, he was delivered up to the Lieutenant of the Towere, where besides the ordinarie miseries incident to that kind of imprisonnement, doubled by the inhumaine dealing and deepe hatred of Catholikes of the cheefe officer there, after sundry examinations, terrors and threattes by the Lord Chauncellor and other of the Counsel and commission, he was divers times racked, to wring out of him by intollerable torments whose houses he frequented, by whom he was reelieved, whom he

The wise lament, the simple grone

He doth reverence to the CROSSE which, in these daies there is odious

Committed to prison in the Tower

The rigor and hatred of the Lieutenant

Often examined & racked.

OF FATHER EDMUND CAMPION 13

had reconciled, what he knewe (a strange case) by their confessions, when, which way, for what purpose, by what commission he came into the Realme, how, where, and by whom he printed and dispersed his bookes and such like. *The interrogatories at his first racking*

At this first racking they went no farther with him, using no great rigor with him in the torment, but afterward when they saw he could not be won to condescende somewhat at least in religion, which they most desired, they thought good to forge matter of treason, and framed their demaundes accordingly, about which he was so cruelly torne and rent upon the torture the two laste times, that he told a secret frend of his that found meanes to speake with him, that he thought they meant to make him away in that sort, and that they demaunded him questions of relieving with money the Irish rebells, of conspiring the Queene's death, invasion of the Realme, and of the sence of certaine wordes of a letter which he wrote to *M. Pound* for answer of his former, which a good fellow promised by othe and his faith (that is the faith of a protestant) receiving an angel for his labour to deliver safely, but did not. The meaning of the wordes he both then and afterward, as well at the barre as at his death, uttered most sincerely, and for the rest, if they had torne him in ten thousand peeces or stilled him to the quintessence, in that holy breast they should never have found any peece of those fained treasons. *The 2 racking, is for forged treasons* *The infidelitie of the Protestant messenger*

He used to fall downe at the rackehowse dore upon both knees to commend him selfe to God's mercie, and to crave His grace of patience in his paines. As also being upon the racke he cried continually with much myldenes upon God and the holy name of Jesus. And when his body was so cruelly distent and streached upon the torment that he did hang by his armes and feete onely, he most charitably forgave his tor- *His usage before he went to the rack.* *His pacience upon the rack* menters and the causers thereof, and thanked one of the rackmen meekely for putting a stone under his backe bone. He said to his keeper after his last racking that it was a preface to death.

And his said keeper asking him the next day how he felt his handes and feet: he answered, 'Not ill, because not at all.' And being in that case benommed both of hand and fote, he likened himselfe to an elephant, which being downe could not rise; when he could hold the bread he had to eate, betwixt both his handes, he would compare himselfe to an ape; so mirry the man of God was in his minde in all his bodely miseries.

Now the ennemies, not contented thus and by many other unwonted waies of torture secretly (as is said) used toward him to afflict his body, but also no lesse by a thousand devilish devises and sclaunderous reportes, sought to wronge him in his fame. Opening all the impure mouthes of the Ministers in London to barke against the man of God; sometimes, that there was great hope he would become a protestant; sometimes, that he had been at the church, and service; an otherwhile, that he had uttered upon the rack all that ever he knew; yea, sometime they blewe out of the Towre that he had therefore killed himselfe in prison, which no doute they would further have avouched, if he had died by racking, as it was like he should have done.

The Lieutenant at the beginning, hoping verely that he might be gayned to their side in some pointes, either by sweete wordes, great promises of promotions or extreme tormens, extolled the man exceedingly, affirming divers times that he was such an one as England never brought furth. 'And suer, (said he), it is God's singular goodnes

His charitie

A pitiful case

The communication betwixt him and his keeper.

He was merrie in God in all his miseries

The Ministers false reports & slaunders of him

The Lieutenant's practise

that he retorned home. No doute her Maiestie will preferre him to great livings.'

And that he might lack no good pretence to yeld unto their desires, they often brought to him such divines as they had, to conferre with him; and to perswade him privatly to relente somwhat to their sect. But not prevailing that way, they caused under coulor of satisfying his former chalenge of disputation, divers publike disputs, or rather certaine light skirmishes, to barke at him and examine him: 4 or 5 of the contrary side, all provided as well as they could, against one voyd of all helps, saving God's grace and lerning: now one snatching and now another, and sometimes all biting togeather, besides the Maisters of the game, that when they saw *F. Campion* in answering and defending himselfe (for he was never suffered to oppose), to gripe the adversaries hard, then they parted them with their tipstaves, commaunding him to silence, and threatening him with lawes, authoritie and punishment. *Protestants brought to conferre with him*

The disorder of their conference. The partialitie used in their disputations

Thus they disputed iij several times with the man of God, shewing nothing in the world, but barbarous despite, malice, and so deepe ignorance in divinitie, that truely divers of the protestants themselves were ashamed thereof, and marveled excedingly at the other's lerning, meekenes, patience and humilitie. But these disputations are to be published, and long sithince should have been; but that, having but hard meanes to print, and few presses and many other bookes in hand, it could not yet be donne. *Their ignorance in divinitie*

And now by this time falling from all hope of his yelding to them, and so from all pitie and good affection towards him, they practised how to make him and his fellowes away by some shew of iustice, and that not for the new made treasons; that is to say, for meere religion, which in truth *No care of religion* few of our adversaries have any care of, but for matters of treason, so called of old, and action against the state, meaning by the state (whatsoever they otherwise pretende) not the preservation of her Maiestie and the weale-publike in deede, which would and might florish, and more securely stand with the Catholike Religion, then by the sect now allowed, but the wealfare of some few raised and upholden by this new religion. Well, they forged matter for their purpose, and to English eares most odible, and found out three or foure false fellowes that would not sticke to swere for their sake the same, against him whom they never knew or saw in their life, before his apprehension. And yeat, fearing lest nothing which they could faine and forge should be hable for any overt act done or past to touch him, they fraudulently sought before hand to seeke his inward intentions and cogitations of future things also, by certaine demaundes concerning the Bull of excommunication put furth against the Queene, or that might be published hereafter, that so at least they might seeme to condemne him for his internal ill affection, whom they could not covinct of any traiterous external fact. So they caused an enditement to be drawen against him and a number more of most godly learned Priests, comprising him and them all in one and together, that whatsoever coulorably might be avouched or witnessed of the rest or any one of them all, either present or absent, all might seeme to the simple and to the Jeury deeply biazed by feare and authoritie, to touch him also with the rest.

The enditement

The 14 day of November *anno* 1581, he and seven others were brought from the towre to the king's beanches barre, and a bille of their enditement read in the hearing of *F. Campion* and the rest. How that in the xxij yere of the

OF FATHER EDMUND CAMPION 17

raigne of our soveraine Lady the Queene, Maij vltimo, in the parties beyond the seas, they had practised the Queene's deposition and death, and the sturring of rebellion within, and invasion of the Realme from abrode, and such like stuffe. Whereupon he was arraigned with the other and commaunded, as custome is in such cases, to hold up his hand. But being pitifully by his often cruel racking benummed before of bothe his armes, and having them wrapped in a furred cuffe, he was not able to lifte his hand so high, nor in that sort as the rest did, and was required of him; one of his fellowes humbly kissing his sacred handes, so wroung for the confession of Christ, tooke of his cuffe, and so he lifted up his arme as highe as he could, pleading not guiltie, as the rest did, and not much standing upon privilege of their cleargie, which they knew in this wicked time in that courte could have no place, he and all the other agreed to be tried by God and their countrey. Wherewith *F. Campion* said, as a true Father, in the behalfe of himselfe and the rest of his children, 'I protest before God and his Angels, before heaven and earth, before the world and this barre whereat I stande, which is but a smale resemblance of the terrible iudgement of the next life, that I am not guiltie thereof, nor of any part of treason contained in the inditement, or of any other treason whatsoever. Again (quoth he) to prove any such thing against me, it is merely impossible.' And then with great admiration and zealous indignation he lifted up his voice, 'Is it possible to find xii so wicked and consciencelesse men in this cityre or land, that will finde us guiltie togeather of this one crime, divers of us never meeting nor knowinge one the other before our bringing to this barre?' And at the same time, when they asked the others severally by whom they would be tried, the blessed

Smale respect of Cleargie now

F. Campion's protestation

confessor *M. Sherwine*, with great courage, clapping his hand upon the barre, answered, that they would be tried 'by God and the countrie, and by all the trials that be in heaven or earth, that God or man hath.' Thus much onely done that day, and a quest was impanelled for the next Munday, being the xx day of the same moneth. But three of the first of that impanel being Squiers, belike fearing God, and doubting that iustice should have no free course that day; but that conscience were like to be put to silence in these men's case, whose bloud was so ernestly thirsted after, those three, I say, appered not. When the day came, *Lye*, Utterbarrester in the Inner Temple, with the rest made their apparance. In the meane time *F. Campion* and his fellow confessors, were recaried to the prisons from whence they came.

They were brought backe againe to iudgement the xx day of Novembre before mentioned; where, notwithstanding what commaundement soever, or order taken to the contrary, there was such a presence of people, and that of the more honorable, wise, lerned and best sort, as was never seen nor heard of in that court, in our, or our fathers' memories before us, or at any arraignement of the greatest dukes or peeres of this land, excepting the number of Lordes, which are there in that case of necessitie; so wonderful an expectation there was of some to see the ende of this marvellous tragedie, contening so many strang and divers acts, of examining, racking, disputing, treacheries, proditions, subornations of false witnesses: and the like of others to behold whether the old honor of law and iustice, wherein our nation hath of all the world had the praise, could or durst stand, notwithstanding any violent impression of power and authoritie to the contrary: whether there were any *Markams* left in the land that would yeld up coiffe, office and life, rather then geve sentence against such as they knew in conscience to be innocent, and in truth not touched by any evidence whatsoever. But this one day gave that assembly and all the world, both present and to come, proffe of the pitieful fall, together with the Catholike Faith of Equitie, law, conscience and iustice, in our poore countrie.

For nothing there said by the Queene's Atturney, Solliciter or other Councellers of that kinde, either by any of those that were at their racking, either by the suborned false witnesses, could in any well enformed man's conscience touch any of them; as every of the rest, and specially this man of God *F. Campion* did, point by point, prove and declare as cleare as the sunne. Yet of all the rest *F. Campion's* innocencie and defence was so plaine in all men's sight, that what coulor soever might be made for the others condemnation, yet for *F. Campion's* none at all. In so much that, whilst the Ieurie were gone furth, divers wise and well lerned lawiers and others, coniecturing and conferring one with another what should be the verdict, they all agreed that it was impossible to condemne *F. Campion*, although some of the rest might upon some sequele be declared guiltie.

But it was *F. Campion* that specially was designed to die, and for his sake the rest. And therefore no defence could serve. The poore xij therefore did that that they thought was loked for at their handes and made them all guiltie, which *M. Popham* told them must needes be found: the uniustest verdict that ever I thinke was geven up in that land, whereat alredy, not onely England, but all the Christian world doth wonder, and all our posteritie shall lament, and be ashamed of the same. Thereupon the sentence of like iniquitie, that all these holy men should be

In Edward 4 his daies

No sufficient proffes brought against them

F. Campion's actions least subiet to calumniations
The iudgement of them that stoode by

They sought specially F. Campion's death
M. Popham gave them a watchword that the Q. would have it founde

hanged, drawen and quartered, after the usual termes of iudgement in the crime of treason, was geven; and so that doleful day was spent. *F. Campion* and his happie associats reioyced in God, using divers holy speaches of scriptures to their owne comforts and other men's much edifying; and so were sent backe to their prisons againe, where, being laied up in yrons for the rest of their time, they expected God's mercie and the Queene's pleasure.

And this blessed *F. Campion* amongest the rest passed his time with such godly spiritual exercises, with such patience and sweete speaches to his keeper and others that had to deale with him, who afterward having the custody of *Norton*, comparing their conditions together said plainely he had before a Sainct in his keeping, and now a Divel, for which speach the plaine spoken man was shent.

And all this while, they still tempted him to their religion, promising life and libertie, notwithstanding his pretended hainous treasons, if he would yeld never so litle unto them; in so much as the Lieutenant said to his sister that came to visite him but iij daies before his Martyrdom, 'If he will yet conforme himself, I will make him spend a hundereth poundes by the yeare.' But his grace and excellencie could not be expugned by such base proffers, the kingdome of England and all the wealth and glorie therein, not being a iust permutation for the least of his vertues, much lesse for his deare soule bought with Christ's pretious bloud, and adorned with God's so singular giftes and graces, the crowne and rewarde whereof he received upon the first of December, as is aforesaid.

The morning that he was brought furth to dye, he met with *M. Sherwin* and *M. Brian* expecting his coming in Coulharbar, where there passed much sweet speach and

margin notes:
The sentence
The good opinion of his keeper
His temptations to yeld
The Lieutenant's proffer to his sister

embrasing one of another: all which while M. Lieutenant sought for *F. Campion's* buffe ierkine, meaning if he could have found it, for the more disgrace of the man of God to have executed him in it; so base is the despiteful malice of such, who with all the persecutors of God's Sainctes, shall be doonge and durte, when these men shall be gloriouse in heaven and earth. When he was brought furthe among the people he said alowde, 'God save you, God bless you all and make you Catholikes.'

The basse and malicious spite of the heretike

And so was caried away to the ordinarie place of execution, and was hanged upon the new gallowes, which is now called among Catholikes the *Gibbet of Martyrs*, because it was first set up and dedicated to the blood of an innocent Catholike Confessor [*D. Storye*], and afterward by this man's, and divers Priests and others' Martyrdoms made sacred.

The Gibbet of martyrs

After he had travailed a good while in the spiritual harvest of our countrey, he wrote this letter folowing of the state thereof to his general.[7]

See Note 7

❡ *Right Reverend Father*

HAVING now passed by God's great mercie five monethes in these places, I thought it good to give you intelligence by my letters of the present stat of things here, and what we may of likelihood looke for to come. For, I am sure, both for your common care of us all and speciall love to me, you long to know what I doe, what hope I have, how I proceede. Of other things that fell before, I wrote from S. Omer's: what have sithence happened, now I will briefly recompt unto you.

It fell out, as I conster it, by God's speciall provision, that tarying for wind four daies together, I should at length take

sea the fifth day in the evening, which was the feast of
S. John Baptist my peculiare patrone to whom I had often
before commended my cause and iourney.

So we arrived safely at Dover the morow folowing very
early, my litle man [*in margin, Litle Raph*] and I together.
There we were at the very point to be taken, being by commaundement brought before the Maior of the towne, who
coniectured many things, suspected us to be such as in deede
we were, adversaries of the new hereticall faction, favorers
of the old fathers' faith, that we dissembled our names, had
ben abroade for religion, and returned againe to spread the
same. One thing he especially urged, that I was *Allen;*
which I denied, profering my othe, if neede were, for the
verefying thereof.

At length he resolveth (and that so it should be, he often
repeated) that, with some to garde me, I should be sent to
the Counsel. Neither can I tell who altered his determina-
tion saving God, to whom underhand I then humbly
praied, using *S. John's* intercession also, by whose happy
helpe I safely came so farre. Sodenly commeth forth an old
man, God give him grace for his labour. 'Well, quoth he, it
is agreed you shall be dismissed. Fare you well.' And so
we two goe apase. The which things considered and the like,
that dailie befal unto me, I am verely persuaded that one
day I shall be apprehended; but that then when it shall
most parteine to God's glorie, and not before.

Well, I came to London, and my good Angel guided
me unwitting into the same howse that had harboured
Father Robert before. Whither yong Gentlemen came
to me on every hand; they embrace me, reapparrel me,
fornish me, weapon me, and convey me out of the
citie.

I ride about some peece of the countrey every day. The harvest is wonderful great. On horse backe I meditate my sermon; when I come to the howse, I poolish it. Then I talke with such as come to speake with me, or heare their confessions. In the morning after Masse I preach.

They heare with exceding greedines, and very often receive the Sacraments; for the ministration whereof we are ever well assisted by Priests, whom we find in every place, whereby both the people is well served, and we much eased in our charge. The priests of our countrey, themselves being most excellent for vertue and learning, yet have raised so great an opinion for our society, that I dare skarcely touch the exceding reverence all Catholikes doe unto us. How much more is it requisite that such as hereafter are to be sent for supplie, whereof we have grete neede, be such as may answere all men's expectation of them. Specially let them be well trained for the pulpit.

I can not long escape the handes of the heretikes; the enemies have so many eies, so many tonges, so many scoutes and crafts. I am in apparell to my self very ridiculouse; I often change it and my name also. I reade letters sometimes my self that in the first front tell newes *That Campion is taken:* which noised in every place where I come, so filleth mine eares with the sound thereof, that feare it self [hath] taken away all feare. *My soule is in my owne handes ever*. Let such as you send for supplie premeditate and make count of this alwaies.

Mary, the solaces that are ever intermedled with these miseries are so great, that they do not only countervaile the feare of what punishment temporal soever, but by infinite sweetnes make all worldly paines (be they never so great) seeme nothing. A conscience pure, a courage invincible, zeale incredible, a worke so worthy, the number innumerable, of high degree, of meane calling, of the inferiour sorte, of every age and sexe. Here even amongest the Protestants them selves that are of mylder nature, it is tourned into a proverb that he must be a Catholike that paieth faithfully that he oweth; in so much that, if any Catholike do inurie, every body expostulateth with him, as for an act unworthie of men of that calling.

To be short, Heresie heareth ill of all men; neither is there any condition of people coumpted more vile and impure then their ministers. And we worthely have indignation that fellowes so unlearned, so evil, so derided, so base, should in so desperate a quarel overrule such a number of noble wittes as our Realme hath.

Threatening edicts come forth against us daily; notwithstanding, by good heede and the praiers of good men and (which is the cheefe of all) by God's special gift, we have passed safely through the most part of the Iland. I find many neglecting their owne securitie, to have only care of my saftie.

A certine matter fell out these daies, by God's appointment, unlooked for. I had set downe in writing by several articles the causes of my comming in, and made certaine demaundes most reasonable. I professed my self to be a Priest of the societie, that I retourned to enlarge the Catholike faith, to teach the Gospel, to minister the Sacraments, humbly asking audience of the Queene and the nobility of the Realme, and proffering disputations to the adversaries. One copie of this writing I determined to keepe with me; that if I should fall into the officers' hands it might goe with me. An other copie I laide in a frendes hand; that when my self with thother should be seazed on, thother might thereupon streight be dispersed.

But my said frend kept it not close longe, but divulged it, and it was redd greedely. Whereat the adversaries were mad, answering out of their pulpits that themselves certes would not refuse to dispute, but the Queene's pleasure was not that matters should be called to question, being already established. In the meane while they teare and stinge us with their venemous tonges, calling us seditious, hypocrites, yea heretikes too, which is much laughed at. The people hereupon is ours, and that error of spreadinge abroade this writting hath much advaunced the cause. Yf we be commaunded and may have safe conduct, we will into the courte.

But they meane nothing lesse; for they have filled all the old prisons with Catholikes, and now make new; and in fine, plainely affirme that it were better to make a few traitors away, then so many soules should be lost.

Of their martyrs they bragge no more now. For it is now come to passe that, for a few apostates and coblers of theirs burned, we have Bishops, Lordes, knightes, the old nobility, paterns of learning pietie and prudence, the flowre of the youth, noble matrones, and of the inferiour sorte innumerable, either martyred at once, or by consuming prisonement dyinge daily. At the very writing hereof the persecution rageth most cruelly. The house where I am is sadd; no other talke, but of death, flight, prison or spoile of their frendes. Nevertheles they proceede with courage.

Very many, even at this present, being restored to the Church, new souldiars geve up their names, whiles the old offer up their blood. By which holy hostes and oblations God will be pleased; and we shall, no question, by him overcome.

You see now, therefore, Reverend Father, how much neede we have of your praiers and sacrifices and other heavenly helpe, to goe through with these thinges. There will never want in England men that will have care of their owne salvation, nor such as shall advance other men's. Neither shall this Church here ever faile, so long as Priests and pastors shall be found for the sheepe: rage man or devil never so much. But the rumor of present perill causeth me here to make an end. *Arise God, his enemies aboide.* Fare you well.

Ed. Camp.

Upon the Death of M. Edmund Campion, one of the Societie of the Holy Name of Iesus [8]

WHY do I use my paper, inke and penne,
And call my wits to counsel what to say?
Such memories were made for Mortall Men,
I speak of Saints whose names can not decaye:
An Angel's trumpe were fitter for to sound
their glorious death, if such on earth wer found.

Pardon my want, I offer nought but will,
their register remaineth safe above.
Campion exceeds the compasse of my skill,
yet let me use the measure of my love,
and give me leave in lowe and homelie verse,
his hye attempts in England to rehearse.

He came by vow: the cause, to conquer sinne.
His armour prayer: the word his targe & shield,
his comfort heaven: his spoyle our soules to win,
the divel his foe, the wicked world the field,
His triumph ioy, his wage eternall blis,
his captaine Christ, which ever blessed is.

From ease to paine, from honour to disgrace,
from love to hate, to daunger being well,
from safe abode to feares in every place,
contemning death to save our soules from hell,
our new Apostle comming to restore
the faith which *Austine* planted here before.

His nature's flowres were mixt with herbes of grace,
his mild behavior tempered well with skill,
a lowly minde possest a learned place,
a sugred speach, a rare & vertuous will.
A saintlike man was set on earth below,
the seede of truth in erring hartes to sow.

With tung & pen the truth he taught & wrote,
by force wherof they came to Christ apace.
But when it pleased God, it was his lote
he should be thrald, He lent him so much grace,
his patience then did worke as much or more
as had his heavenly speeches done before.

His fare was hard, yet mild & sweet his cheere,
his prison close, yet free & lose his minde,
his torture great, yet small or none his feare,
his offers large, but nothing could him blinde.
O constant man, O mind, O vertue strange,
Whom want, nor wo, nor feare, nor hope coulde change.

From racke in Tower they brought him to dispute,
bookeles, alone, to answere all that came,
Yet Christ gave grace, he did them all confute
so sweetly there in glory of his name,
that even the advers part are forst to say
that *Campion's* cause did beare the bell away.

This foyle enraged the minds of some so farre,
they thought it best to take his life away,
because they saw he would their matter marre,
and leave them shortly nought at all to say:
traytor he was with many and seely slight,
Yet pact a Iury that cried guilty straight.

Religion there was treason to the Queene,
preaching of penance warre against the lande,
priests were such dangerous men as have not bin,
Prayers & beads were fight & force of hande,
cases of conscience bane unto the state.
So blind is error, so false a witnes hate.

And yet behold these lambes be drawen to dye,
treason proclaymed, the queene is put in feare,
out upon Satan, fye malice, fye,
Speakst thou to them that did the guiltles heare?
Can humble soules departing now to Christ,
protest untrue? Avant, foule fend, thou lyst.

My soveraigne Liege, behold your subiects end,
your secret foes do misenforme your grace:
Who in your cause their holy lives would spend,
as traytors dye, a rare & monstrous case.
The bloudy wolfe condemns the harmles shepe,
before the dog, ye whiles the shepherds slepe.

England looke up, thy soyle is stained with blood,
thou hast made martirs many of thine owne,
if thou hast grace their deaths will do thee good,
the seede will take, which in such blood is sowne,
and *Campion's* lerning fertile so before,
thus watered too, must nedes of force be more.

Repent thee *Eliot* of thy *Judas* kisse,
I wish thy penance, not thy desperate ende,
let *Norton* thinke, which now in prison is,
to whom was said he was not *Cæsar's* friend,
and let the Judge consider well in feare,
that *Pilate* washt his hands, and was not cleare.

Ye witnes false, *Sledd, Munday* & the rest,
which had your slanders noted in your booke,
confesse your fault beforehand it were best,
Lest God do find it written when he doth looke
in dreadfull doome upon the soules of men,
it will be late (alas) to mend it then.

You bloody iury, *Lea* and all the leaven,
take heede your verdit which was given in haste,
do not exclude you from the joys of heaven,
and cause you rue it, when the time is past:
and every one whose malice causd him say
Crucifige! let him dread the terror of that day.

Fonde *Elderton*[9] call in thy foolish rime,   *See Note* 9
thy scurile balates are too bad to sell,
let good men rest, and mende thyself in time,
confesse in prose thou hast not meetred well.
Or if thy folly can not choose but fayne,
write alehouse toys, blaspheme not in thy vain.

Remember you that would oppresse the cause,
the Church is Christe's, his honor can not dye,
though hell herselfe reuest her gresly jawes,
and joyne in league with schisme and heresie,
though craft devise, and cruel rage oppresse,
yet skill will write and martirdome confesse.

You thought perhaps when lerned *Campion* dyes,
his pen must cease, his sugred tong be still;
but you forgot how lowde his death it cryes,
how farre beyond the sound of tongue and quill.
You did not know how rare & great a good
it was to write his precious giftes in blood.

Living he spake to them that present were,
his writings took their censure of the viewe,
Now fame reports his lerning farre & nere,
and now his death confirmes his doctrine true.
His vertues now are written in the skyes,
and often read with holy inward eyes.

All Europe wonders at so rare a man,
England is fild with rumor of his ende,
London must needs for it was present than,
When constantly three saints their lives did spend.
The streets, the stones, the steps you hald them by,
proclaime the cause for which these Martirs dy.

The Tower saith the truth he did defend,
the barre beares witnes of his guiltles minde,
Tiborne doth tell he made a pacient ende,
on every gate his martirdome we finde,
in vaine you wroght, that would obscure his name
for heaven & earth will still record the same.

Your sentence wrong pronounced of him here,
exempts him from the judgement for to come;
O happy he that is not judged there!
God graunt me too to have an earthly doom,
Your witnes false & lewdly taken in,
doth cause he is not now accused of sin.

His prison now the citie of the king,
his racke & torture joyes & heavenly blisse,
for men's reproach with angels doth he sing
A sacred song which everlasting is.
For shame but short & loss of small renowne
he purchased hath an ever during crowne.

His quarterd lims shall joyne with joy againe,
and rise a body brighter than the sunne,
Your blinded malice torturde him in vayne,
for every wrinch some glory hath him wonne,
And every drop of blood which he did spend,
hath reapt a joy which never shall have end.

Can dreary death then daunt our faith, or paine?
Is't lingering life we feare to loose, or ease?
No, no, such death procureth life againe,
'tis only God we tremble to displease,
Who kills but once, and ever still we dye,
Whose hote revenge tormentes eternallye.

We can not feare a mortal torment, wee,
this Martir's blood hath moystened all our harts,
whose partid quartirs when we chaunce to see,
we lerne to play the constant christian's parts.
His head doth speak, & heavenly precepts give,
how we that look should frame our selves to live.

His youth enstructes us how to spend our daies,
his flying bids us how to banish sinne,
his straight profession shows the narrow waies
which they must walk that looke to enter in.
his home returne by danger and distresse,
emboldens us our conscience to professe.

His hardle drawes us with him to the crosse,
his speeches there provoke us for to dye,
his death doth say this life is but a losse,
his martired blood from heaven to us doth crye,
his first and last and all conspire in this,
to shew the way that leadeth unto blisse.

Blessed be God which lent him so much grace,
thanked be Christ which blest his Martirs so,
happy is he which sees his Master's face,
Cursed are they that thought to work him wo,
bounden be we to give eternall prayse,
to Jesus name which such a man did rayse.

    Amen.

A Dialogue betwene a Catholike and Consolation

Catholike first speaketh.

IS righteous *Lot* from sinful Sodome gone?
is olde *Elias* left alone agayne?
and hath the earth no just man, no not one,
the cause of Christ & Christians to sustaine?
if holy life with true religion fayle,
then farewell faith, for falsehood will prevayle.

Consolation

No, *Lot*, thou hast some felowes in this lande.
Elias, there are left seven thousand yet,
rejoice thou earth thou hast a warlike bande,
for our good Lord in martial order set,
by life & death this quarrel to beginne
to vanquish falsehood, satan, hell and sinne.

although a worthy Champion of your trayne
were slain of late, and yet not vanquished,
into his place another stept againe,
whom Christ's spouse our common nurse hath bred.
Lament not then, for there are in his rome
as good as he, expecting martirdome.

Catholike

Such men no doubt are very hard to finde,
for dainty things are seldome sifted out,
the Phenix hath no partner of her kinde
a man perhaps may seeke the world about,
ere he may find one *Campion* agayne,
wherfore his losse makes me the more complaine.

Where shall you find so many giftes in one,
a wit so sharpe, joyned with such memory,
a great divine hating promotion,
a lusty man possessing chastitie,
a worthy impe sprong up of basest kind,
a lerned man to beare a lowly mind.

Solon for pith, for wisedome *Salomon*,
Peter for style, & *Paule* for eloquence,
David for truth, for beautie *Absolon*,
for personage *Saule*, a *Iobe* for patience:
All that for which the fame of these began,
(a thing most strange) were ioyned in this one man.

Not racke, nor rope coold daunt his dredles mind,
no hope nor hap could move him where he stood,
he wrote the truth as in his bookes we finde,
which to confirme he sealed with his blood,
which makes me dout there are no mo such men.
Send workmen Lord into thy vineyarde then.

Consolation

Despair thou not, thou seely mournful wight,
for there are mo have tooke this match in hand.

We needs must win, our Lord himselfe doth fight,
the Cananites shall be expulsd the land,
for *Edmund* lives and helpeth godly men
by prayers more than erst with tongue or pen.

His quarters hong on every gate do showe,
his doctrine found through countries far & neare,
his head set up so high doth call for moe
to fight the fight which he endured here,
the faith thus planted, thus restord must be.
Take up thy crosse, saith Christ, & folow me.

As well as priests the lay men too shall frame,
their skillesse heads to take so good a vowe,
God can of stones raise seede to Abraham,
doubt not therefore, for there will be enowe.

Catholike

Fiat voluntas Dei then say I,
We owe a death, and once we needes must dye.

FINIS

M. RALPH SHERWINE
Priest & Master of Arts

Chap. II

M. Sher-wine's spiritual exercises

FATHER CAMPION having so gloriously triumphed over the world, the flesh, the divel and Heresie and received his long desired crowne, *M. Raph Sherwine*, a godly, wise, discreet and lerned priest, was brought into the carte, a man so mortified, so feebled with fasting, watching and such other spiritual exercises, as was wonderful unto such who had conversed with him before his imprisonment.

His behaviour in the carte

He standing upon the carte, with closed eyes, with handes lifted up to heaven in contemplation and praier, all men marking his demeanur, with milde voice first made this demaund: *Doth the people expect that I should speake?* Being answered of many and some of nobilitie, 'Yea, yea'; with stoute courage and strong voice he said, 'Then first, I thanke the omnipotent and most merciful God the Father for my creation, my sweete and loving Saviour Jesus Christ for my redemption, and the Holy Ghost for my sanctification; three Persons and one God.'

After this thankes-geving unto the holy and blessed Trinitie, entring into the discourse of his faith, his condemnation and death, he was interrupted & staid by *Sir*

OF FATHER EDMUND CAMPION 35

Francis Knowles and the Sherifes, saying, 'You have declared your faith, and we know it. Come to the point, and confesse your treason and disloyaultie towards your Prince.' Whereupon he constantly said, '*I am innocent and guiltles.*' And being still urged, answered, '*I will not belie myself, for so should I condemne my owne soule.*' And although I have confusion in this world, yet I doubt not of my salvation in Christ Jesus, in whom only I looke to be saved, and in whose death, Passion and bloud I only trust.' And so he made a sweete praier to Jesus, acknowledging the imperfection, miserie, and sinful wretchedness of his owne nature, still protesting his innocencie from all Treasons and traiterous practises, & that his going out of this Realme beyond the seas was only for his soule's health, to learn to save his soule.

And being againe interrupted by *Sir Francis Knowles* he answered in this wise, '*Tush, tush! You and I shall answere this before another Iudge, where my innocencie shall be knowen, and you see that I am guiltles of this.*' Whereupon *Sir Frauncis* said, 'We knowe you are no contriver or doer of this treason for you are no man of armes, *but you are a traitor by consequence.*'

But *M. Sherwine* boldly answered, '*If to be a Catholike onely; if to be a perfect Catholike be to be a traitor, then am I a traitor.*' After which wordes being by authoritie debarred of further speech, he said, '*I forgeve all who either by general presumption or particular error have procured my death,*' and so devoutely praied unto Jesus. After which praier he was urged to speak his opinion touching *Pope Pius* his Bull, to which point he gave no answere.

Being willed to pray for the Q.Maiestie he answered, '*I have and do.*' At which wordes the *L. Howard* againe

margin notes:
Innocencie
The cause of his going beyond the seas
By consequence quoth he?
His charitie
They baite this bull wonderfully

asked which Queene he meant, whether Elizabeth Queene? To whom somewhat smiling he said, '*Yea, for* Elizabeth Queene, *I nowe at this instant pray my Lord God to make her his servant in this life, and after this life coheir with Christ Jesus.*'

When he had thus praied, there were there which said openly that he ment to make her a Papist, to whom he boldly replied, '*Els God forbid.*' And so collecting himselfe to praier, died, paciently, constantly and mildely, crying, '*Jesus, Jesus, Jesus! Esto mihi Jesus.*'

Thus this blessed man was delivered of this corruptible body, of whose life I thought good to set downe some few lines also. He was a Master of Arte, and so well learned that he was Senior of his act or commencement, which is a schole charge of honor, and done by him in the presence of the *Earl of Leicester* and divers others of the nobilitie that came from the court then lying at Wodstocke, to their great liking and his commendation. He was also very skilful in the three tongues [Hebrew, Greek and Latin].[10] Leaving the universitie, and the condition he had in his colledg for conscience sake, he went over to *Doway* to the Seminarie that was then there, and after some yeres study in divinitie was made priest the xxiij of March the yere M.D.LXXVII together with *M. Lawrence Johnson*, that was martyred under the name of *Richardson*. The ij day of August the same yere he was sent to Rome in company with *M.* [*Rishton*], who was condemned with him also. There he studied in the Seminarie till the yere M.DLXXX, at what time he retorned homeward, and came to Remes, where he staied certaine daies after his fellowes (who then by divers waies and portes were entered into the Realme) upon this occasion.

He smileth at their follie

A hainous treason to wish the Q saluation

His life

Senior in the act

And skilful in the tongues.

See Note 10

Left the universitie, went to Douay

Was made priest

He went to Rome

OF FATHER EDMUND CAMPION 37

There was not long before special sute made to his Holines, that as we had of priests to all spiritual purposes good store for our countrey, so we might have at least one Suffragane or Bishop to supplie divers necessarie functions that could not be done by the inferior cleargie, as amongest other things the Sacrament of Confirmation, which, being specially ordained of our Saviour to geve strength and constancie to stand in defence of the faith in such times of persecution as this is, was much necessarie for our countrey, and could not be had, by reason all our true bishops were either dead, in prison, or so restrained that they could not exercise that, or other their holy Ministeries. *A motion made to the Pope of a suffragane for England* *Great lacke of Confirmation*

The Pope, though he deliberated thereupon some daies, yet in the end, upon very many wise considerations, and specially for that he would not have any of that high calling fall into the hands of the ennemy, not doubting but that they would use such an one as barbarously as any other Priest or Catholike, did not thinke it good at that time to create any such. *Causes why the Pope would not graunt it*

But afterward the right Reverend in God *Thomas Goldwell, Bishop of S. Assaph*, a most Venerable and aunciente Confessor, that hath suffered banishment for his conscience halfe his life, though he be well nere lxxx yeres of age, hearing the marvelous zeale of so many godly Priests, and their heroical endevours for the salvation of their countrey, was sturred in spirit, and much desired to end the remnant of his old yeres in the service of his countrey, & went to his Holines to desire his leave and benediction in that behalfe: and with much adoe, for that great respect was had of his dignitie and his old age, it was graunted him. *The cause why the Bishop of S. Assaph came out of Italy*

Whereupon the old honorable Father adventured downe as fare as Rhemes in all the heats, where he gave to the

Seminarie the greatest comfort, and the same yelded to him all the contentement in the world. There he consulted how to gaine our countrey to salvation by any office of life, or by glad suffering of death itself.

What the Counsel imagined of his and others coming downe

Which meeting, and specially that old and Reverend Confessor's comming downe for England as they all deemed, put marvelous concepts into the Counsel's heads, that there was some great and newe attempt of invasion toward. For worldly men standing only at the watch of the temporal state could not imagine that for gaining of a soule or two, or for conversion of a kingdom either, such men would be so diligent and venturous as to come upon their pickes and ropes without some worldly succours.

The cause of the Bishops stay and retorne

Now it so chanced by God's providence that the said L. of S. Assaph for other causes, and specially for that he fell into a very daungerous ague with the contagious cough which then raigned in Rhemes, he could not passe on in his iorney so spedeley as other of the Societie and Priests did. Wherefore for his more honor & comfort some other, and specially this man of God *M. Sherwine*, offered to tarie with his Lordship during his sicknes, and then, when God should send him strength, to be one of his chapliens and conductors into his countrey. But it was resolved at length that for the uncertentie of his recovery *M. Sherwine* should passe forward toward Roan, and there rather to expect him, as he did.

But the good Father, now much weakened by his sickenes, and otherwise not well appointed, nor in deed fit for to take the paines, nor any waies, by reason of his markeable person, very great age, and feebleness, long like to escape the persecutors' hands, was in fine altered from that purpose, and after his recovery he thought good rather to retorne into Italie againe, as he did.

And *M. Sherwine* went forward towards England, where after his arrival he occupied himself in all functions belonging to the Priesthod, with great zeale and charitie, and sone after he was taken in *M. Roscarroke's* chamber in London, and committed to the Marshalsey, where he lay night and day in a great paire of shakles for the space of a moneth. *His apprehension* · *How he was used in prison*

In November after his imprisonment, there came word from the *Knight Marshal* to the keeper of the Marshalsey, to understand of him, whether there were any Papists in his prison that durst or would maintaine their cause by disputation; and if there were any such, that then they should send him such questions as they would defend, subscribed with their handes, and make them ready to dispute, for they should understand from him shortely, of the manner, time and place, how and where to dispute. *A motion of disputations*

This notion was so well liked of the Catholikes, that this *M. Sherwine* and two other Priests that were condemned with him afterwards, *M. Hart* & *M. Bosgrave*, offered themselves to the combat, drewe out questions, subscribed their names, and sent them to the said *K. Marshal*. But their questions pleasing him not, they do accept and allowe of other questions sent unto them from the said *K. Marshal*, and do expect with joyful minde the day appointed to dispute. *Accepted by the Catholikes*

But loe, even the day before they should have disputed, *M. Sherwine* was removed to the Tower where he was at sundrie & several times examined and racked. *He is removed to the Tower*

In his first racking he was asked where *F. Campion* and *F. Parsons* were, why he and they came over into England, what acquaintance he had here in England, whether he said Masse in *M. Roskaroke's* chamber, and whether he had of him at any time money. He was close prisoner al- *His racking and the interrogatories*

THE DEATH & MARTYRDOM

His conference with the Ministers did much good

most a whole yere, in which time he had divers conferences with ministers both privately, and in some open audience both of honorable and worshipful, to the honor of God, the benefit of his afflicted church, and to the admiration of most of the hearers. He was after his first racking, set out in a great snow, and laid upon the racke, and the Gentilman in whose chamber he was taken, was kept in a bye darck corner to heare his pitiful grones and complaints.

Great crueltie

He was delt withal to goe to the schismatical church

On Midsomer-day in the yere 1581, he was called before the Lieutenant (as likewise all his fellow prisoners were) who demaunded of him by commision from the Counsel, whether he would goe to their heretical service; who refusing, the Lieutenant told him the danger of a late statute made in that behalfe, and that farther he should be endited upon that statute within ij or iij daies, so that at that time, as it should seeme, they had no such matter to lay against him as after was pretended, for it was not as then throughly hatched."

The treason as then not hatched

See Note 11

Even the Protestants did admire his vertues

The order of his life in his spare diet, his continual praier and meditation, his long watching, with ofte and sharpe discipline used upon his body, caused great admiration to his keeper, who would alwaies call him, *a man of God*, and the best and devoutest priest that ever he saw in his life.

His notable speach to F. Campion

When he came out of the Lieutenant's hall (with other of his fellowes) two daies or there about before he was martyred, having talked with a minister who was never so holden up to the wall in his life, (by report of such as stoode by) he uttered these wordes, '*Ah, F. Campion, I shall be shortely above yonder fellow*,' pointing to the sunne, with such a courage that some said he was the resolutest man that ever they saw.

OF FATHER EDMUND CAMPION   41

He will never be forgotten in the Tower for some wordes which he spake when he was ready to goe to execution, attending *F. Campion* who was lodged further of. *Charke* the minister can best report them, who stoode hard by him. Some of *Charke's* fellow ministers said, those wordes could not come from a guiltie conscience.

The very Ministers iudge him innocent

⁋ *The Copie of a Letter written out of the Tower by M. Sherwine to his frendes*

iij or iiij *of the latter lines are wanting*

BEING wearie of well doing,[12] and yet desirous not to do nothing (my deare companions), I chose rather by writting unto you to performe my deutie then otherwise to recreate my head with cogitations lesse necessarie.

See Note 12

Your liberalitie I have received, and disposed thereof to my great contentation. When hereafter at the pleasure of God we shall meet in heaven, I trust you shall be repaied *cum foenore*. Delay of our death doth somewhat dull me. It was not without cause that our Maister himselfe said, *Quod facis fac cito*.

Truth it is I hoped ere this, casting off this body of death, to have kissed the pretious glorified woundes of my sweete Saviour, sitting in the throne of his Father's owne glorie. Which desire, as I trust descending from above, hath so quieted my minde that since the Iudicial sentence proceded against us, neither the sharpnes of the death hath much terrified me, nor the shortnes of life much troubled me. My sinnes are great I confesse, but I flee to God's mercie; my necligences are without number I graunt, but I appeale to my Redeemer's clemencie. I have no bouldnes but in His bloud; His bitter passion is my only consolation. It is comfortable that the Prophet hath recorded, which is, that *he hath written us in his handes.* Oh, that he would vouchsaffe to writ himself in our harts, how joyful should we then appeare before the tribunal seat of His Father's glorie. The dignitie whereof when I thinke, my flesh quaketh, not sustaining by reason of mortal infirmitie the presence of my Creator's Majestie.

Our Lord perfect us to that ende whereunto we were created, that leaving this world, we may live in Him, and of Him, World without ende. It is thought that upon Munday or Tewsday next we shall be passible, God graunt us humilitie, that we following His footsteps may obteine the victorie.

⁋ *Another Letter written by him the day before his Martyrdom, to his Uncle M. John Wood-*
ward, a Venerable Priest
abiding at Roan

Absit ut gloriemur,
nisi in Cruce Domini Jesu Christi.

MY dearest uncle, after many conflicts and worldly cor-rasies,[13] mixed with spiritual consolations, and Christian comfortes, it hath pleased God of his unspeakable mercie to call me out of this vale of miserie. To him therefor for all his benefits at all times and for ever, be all praise and glorie.

Your tender care alwaies had over me, and cost bestowed on me I trust in heaven shall be rewarded. My praiers you have still had, and that was but deutie. Other tokens of a grateful minde I could not shew by reason of my restrained necessitie.

See Note 13

This very morning, which is the festival day of *S. An-drew*, I was advertised by superior authoritie, that to-morrow I was to ende the course of this life. God graunt I may do it, to the imitation of this noble Apostle and ser-vant of God, & that with ioy I may say rising off the herdle, '*Salve sancta Crux*. O bona crux, quæ decorem ex membris Domini suscepisti, diu desiderata, solicite amata, sine intermissione quæsita, & aliquando cupienti animo præparata. Accipe me ab hominibus, & redde me magistro meo, vt per te me recipiat, qui per te me redemit.' Inno-cencie is my only comfort, against all the forged villanie which is fathred on my fellow Priests and me. Well, when by the high Judge, God himself, this false visard of treason shall be removed from true Catholike men's faces, then shall it appeare who they be that carry a well meaning, and who an evil murdering minde. In the meane season God forgeve all iniustice; and, if it be His blessed will to convert our persecutors, that they may become professors of His truth.

Praiers for my soule procure for me my loving patrone, and so having great neede to prepare myself for God, never quieter in minde, nor lesse troubled towards God, bynding all my iniquities up in his precious woundes. I bid you *Farewell*, yea and once againe to the lovingest uncle that ever kinsman had in this world, *Farewell*.

God graunt us both His grace and blessing until the ende, that living in His feare and dying in His favour, we may enioy one the other for ever. And so my good old John, *farewell*. Salute all my fellow Catholikes, and so without farther troubling of you, my sweetest benefactor *farewell*. On *S. Andrewe's* day 1581.

Your cosen,
Raph Sherwine, Priest.

The complaynt of a Catholike for the death of M. Edmund Campion [and his companions]

O GOD from sacred throne behold
   our secret sorrows here,
Regard with grace our helplesse griefe,
   amend our mournful cheere.
The bodies of our Saints abrode
   are set for foules to feede,
And brutish birds devour the flesh
   of faithful folke in deede.

Alas, I rue to thinke upon
   the sentence truely scande,
No prophet any honour hath
   within his native lande.
Thy dolefull death, O *Campion*, is
   bewalyd in every coste,
But we live here & little knowe
   what creatures we have loste.
Bohemia land laments the same,
   Rodulphus' court is sad,
With deep regarde they now recorde
   What vertues *Campion* had.
Germania Mourns, all Spayne doth Muse,
   and so doth Italy,
And Fraunce, our friend, hath put in print
   his passing tragedie.

They that would make these men to seeme
   to be her highnes' foes,
O Lorde it is a world to see
   the fayned fraude of those.
For when they had in dastard wise
   devised to dispute,
And could not finde in all their craft
   the cause for to confute;

And that their winnings was so [small],
    they needed not to boste,
And that in consciens they did know
    new found is lightly loste;
They suttly seeke a further fetche
    contrary to all reason,
To say he is not *Cæsar's* frende,
    accusing him of treasone.

But shall we mutche lament the same
    or shall we more rejoyce?
Such was the case with Christ our Lord,
    sutche was the Jewish voyce.
So wer their wrathful words pronounst,
    so was their sentence wrong,
For Christ did give to *Cæsar* that
    which did to him belong.
So Christ his true disciples here
    no treason do pretend,
But they by Christ & Christ his lore
    their fayth till death defende.

Though error have devised now
    A visard so unfit
To cloke her craft to change the case
    to blear each simple wit,
Because she taught us long before
    that none for poynts of fayth
According un'to Christe's lore
    ought to be done to death.
Her wilines wer soone bewrayed,
    had they but once recanted;
No doubt thereof they had not then
    nor life nor living wanted.
Thus whoso weighs her works & words
    with fraude shall find them fraught,
And how they now perform the same
    that heretofore they taught.

God knowes it is not force nor might,
  not warre nor warlike band,
Not shield & spear, not dint of sword,
  that must convert the land,
It is the blood by martirs shed,
  it is that noble traine,
That fight with word & not with sword,
  and Christ their capitaine.
For sooner shall you want the handes
  to shed such guiltles blood,
Then wise and vertuous still to come
  to do theyr country good.

God save Elizabeth our queene,
  God send her happie raigne,
And after earthly honors here,
  the heavenly ioyes to gayne.
And all sutch men as heretofore
  have misinformed her Grace,
God graunt they may amend the same
  while here they have the space.

FINIS

OF M. ALEXANDER BRIAN
Priest and Graduat

Chap. III

AFTER these two glorious Martyrs was brought unto his Martyrdome *M. Alexander Brian*, a man not unlerned, of a very sweete grace in preaching, but of passing zeale, patience, constancie & humilitie, of whose pressures in prison and tortures (strange I dare say among heathens, more monstruous among Christians) I will speake anone.

Being in the carte prepared to death, he begane first to declare his bringing up in the Catholike faith and religion, his being in Oxford. Upon which word he was staid by one saying: 'What haue we to do with Oxford? Come to the purpose and confesse thy treason.' Whereupon he answered, '*I am not guiltie of any such death. I was never at Rome; nor then at Remes, when D. Saunders came into Irland.*' To this ende he spake and protested, as he would answer before God.

He spake not much, but whereas he was urged more than the others to speake what he thought of the said *Bull* of *Pius Quintus*, he said he did beleeve of it as all Catholikes and the Catholike faith doth, and thereupon protest-

M. Brians rare giftes

Innocence

This Bull is stil revived

ing himselfe to die a true Catholike. As he was saying *Miserere mei, Deus,* he was delivered of the carte with more pain by necligence of the hangman than either of the other, who after his beheading, himself dismembred, his hart, bowels and intrailes burned, to the great admiration of some, being laid upon the block his belly downward, lifted up his whole body then remayning from the ground: and this I adde upon report of others, not mine owne sight.

Of this man's life we will not speake, though it was alwaies for all vertue & grace most spectable, but adde onely a few wordes of the things that he endured for his faith in the time of his imprisonment.

He is taken & his chamber riffled

About the 28 of April he was apprehended in his chamber at midnight by *Norton,* his chamber riffled, three poundes of money taken from him (for that is a principal verbe in all apprehensions of Catholikes), his apparel and other things, especially a trunke wherein was a silver chalice, and much other good stuffe, which was not his but committed to his custodie, taken away also, and he sent close prisoner to the Counter, with commaundement to stay all that asked for him, & that he should have neither meat nor drinke, and

He was almost famished

he continued in such order until he was almost famished. In fine by friendship or what meanes I know not, he gott a peny worth of hard cheese and a little broken bread, with a pinte of strong beare, which brought him into such an extreme thirst that he assaied to take with his hatte the dropps of raine from the house eeves, but could not reach them.

He is removed to the Tower His feare of famine there

The morrow after the Ascension day he was removed to the Tower, where he verely thought he should have been utterly famished, and therefore caried with him a little peece of his hard cheese, which his keeper in searching him found about him, but *M. Brian* humblie entreated his keeper not to take it from him. His ordinarie allowance in drinke, which was at every meale a potel-pot full, could not for a great while suffice him, such was his exceding thirst. *See Note 14*

Within two daies after his comming to the Tower he was brought before the *Lieutenant*, M. D. *Hammon*, and *Norton*, who examined him after their common maner, first in tendering an othe to answere to all, etc. And because he would not confess where he had seene *F. Parsons*, how he was manteined, where he had said *Masse*, and whose confessions he had heard, they caused needles to be thrust under his nailes, whereat M. *Brian* was not moved at all, but with a constant minde and plesant countenance said the Psalme *Miserere*, desiring God to forgive his tormentors. Whereat D. *Hammon* stampt & stared, as a man half beside himselfe, saying, 'What a thing is this, if a man were not setled in his religion this were inough to convert him.' *His examination* *A cruel kind of torment*

He was even to the dismembring of his body rent and torne upon the rack, because he would not confess where *F. Parsons* was, where the print was, & what bookes he had sould, and so was returned to his lodging for that time. *He was pitifully racked*

Yet the next day following, notwithstanding the great distemperature and soreness of his whole body, his senses being dead, and his bloud congealed (for this is the effect of racking), he was brought to the torture againe, and there stretched with greater severitie than before (supposing with himself, that they would plucke him in pieces, and to his thinking there was a vaine broken in his hand, and that bloud ishued out there a pase) he put on the armor of patience, resolving to dye rather than to hurt any *He is racked againe almost to death* creature living, and having his minde raised in contemplation of Christ's bitter Passion, he swoond,[15] so that they were faine to sprinckle cold water on his face to revive him againe, yet they released no part of his paine.

And here *Norton*, because they could get nothing of him, asked him, whether the Queene were supreme head of the Church of England or not, to this he said, '*I am a Catholike, and I believe in this as a Catholike should do.*' 'Why, said *Norton*, they say the Pope is [head of the Church].' 'And so say I,' answered *M. Brian*. Here also the Lieutenant used railing and reviling words, and bobd[16] him under the chinne, and slapt him on the cheekes after an uncharitable maner. And all the commissioners rose up and went their way, giving commaundement to leave him so all night. At which when they saw he was nothing moved, they willed that he should be taken from the torment, and sent him again to *Walesboure*, where not able to move hand nor fote or any part of his body, he lay in his clothes xv daies together without bedding in great paine and anguish.

When he went to Westminster hall to be condemned, he made a Crosse of such wood as he could gett, which he carried with him openly. He made shifte also to shave his crowne, because he wold signify to the prating Ministers (which scoffed and mocked him at his apprehension, saying that he was ashamed of his vocation) that he was not ashamed of his holy orders, nor yet that he would blush at his religion. When he was condemned, yrons were commaunded upon him, and the rest, as sone as they came home to the Tower, and they were never taken off, till they were fetched furth to be martyred.

These torments and the man's constancie are comparable truly to the old strange suffering of the renommed Mar-

---

See Note 15

The Pope not the Queene is head of the Church So was Christ, & S. Paul used by the like men

See Note 16

This is a terrible dongeon

He was not ashamed of his Masters Badge

OF FATHER EDMUND CAMPION 51

tyrs of the primitive Church in the daies of *Nero, Decius* and *Diocletian*, which he could never have borne by humane strength, if God had not given him singular & supernatural grace. Himself confessed that by a vow he made & other special exercises, he had a great consolation in all these vexations, whereof I will set down his own wordes in an Epistle that he wrot to the Fathers of the Societie in England.[17]

See Note 17

¶ M. BRIAN'S EPISTLE TO THE FATHERS OF THE SOCIETIE

[*Reverend Fathers in Christ,*
Pax Christi

MORE than two years ago I resolved, if it were God's will that I should return to foreign parts, that I would embrace the mode of life of congregations dedicated to God, and seek admission among the Fathers of the Societie. But because I hoped that my labour & industry in the harvest of our Lord would not be altogether useless, I deferred the proposal, though I have very frequently renewed my resolution during these two years, which I have lived in England.] Yet now, sith I am by the appointment of God deprived of libertie, so as I cannot any longer employe myselfe in this profitable exercise, my desire is eftsones revived, my spirit waxeth fervent hote, and at the last I have made a vow and promise to God, not rashly (as I hope) but in the feare of God, not to any other ende then that I might therby more devoutly and more acceptably serve God, to my more certain salvation, and to a more gloriouse triumphe over my ghoostlie enemie. I have made a vow (I say) that whensoever it shall please God to deliver me (so that once at the length it like Him) I will, within one year then next following, assigne my selfe wholy to the fathers of the societie, and that (yf God inspire their harts to admit me) I will gladly, and with exceding great joy throwly and from the bottom of my hart give up and surrender all my will to the service of God, and in all obedience under them.

This vow was to me a passing great ioye, and consolation in the myddes of all my distresses, and tribulations. And therefore with greater hope to obtein fortitude and patience, I drew near to the throne of his divine majestie, with the assistance of the blessed and perpetual virgin Marie, and of all the Sainéts. And I hope verily this came of God, for I did it even in the time of praier, when me thought my minde was settled upon heavenly things. For thus it was.

The same day that I was first tormented on the rack before I came to the place, giving my mind to praier, and commending my selfe and all mine to oure Lorde, I was replenished, and filled up with a kinde of supernatural swetenesse of spirit. And even while I was calling upon the most holie name of Jesus, and upon the blessed virgin Marie (for I was in saying the Rosarie) my mind was cheerfully disposed, well comforted, and readily prepared and bent to suffer and endure those torments which even then I most certainly looked for. At the length my former purpose came into my minde, and there withall a thought coincidentlly fell upon me to ratifie that now by vowe, which before I had determined. When I had ended my praiers, I resolved these things in my minde deeply, and with reason (as well as I could) I did debate and discusse them thorowly; I judgd it good, and expedient for me; I accomplished my desire: I put forth my vow and promise freely and boldly, with the condition afore saide.

Which acte (me thinketh) God himself did approve and allow by and by. For in all my afflictions and torments he of his infinite goodnesse, mercifully and tenderly, did stand by and assiste me, comforting me in my trouble and necessitie. *Delivering my soule from wicked lipps, from the deceitful tongue and from the roring lyons* then readie gaping for their pray.

Whether this that I will say be miraculous or no, God he knoweth: but true it is, and thereof my conscience is a witnesse before God, and this I say, that in the end of the torture, though my handes and feete were violently stretched and racked, and my adversaries fulfilled their wicked lust, in practisinge their cruell tyranny upon my body, yet notwithstanding, I was without sense and feeling well nigh of all greefe and paine: and not so only, but as it were comforted, eased and refreshed of the greeves of the torture bypast, I continued still with perfect and present senses, in quietnes of hart, and tranquilitie of mind. Which thing when the commissioners did see, they departed, and in going foorth of the doore they gave order to racke me againe the next day following after the same sorte. Now, when I hearde them say so, it gave me in my mind by and by, and I did verely believe and trust, that with the help of God I should be able to beare and suffer it patiently. In the mean time (as well as I could), I did muse and meditate upon the moste bitter passion of oure Saviour, and how full of innumerable paines it was. And whiles I was thus occupied, me thought that my left hand was wounded in the palme, and that I felt the blood runne out, but in very deede there was no such thing, nor any other paine then that which seemed to be in my hand.

Now then that my sute and request may be well knowne

unto you, for so much as I am oute of hope in short time to recouer and enioye my former libertie so as I might personally speake unto yow. And whether happely I shall once at length speake unto yow in this world no mortall man doeth know. In the meane season I humbly submitt my selfe unto yow, and (suppliantly kneeling) I beseche yow to doe, and dispose for me, and of me, as shall seeme good to youre wisdoms; and with an humble mind moste hartilie I crave that (if it may be in my absens) it would please yow to admit me into your Societie, and to regester and inrole me among yow, that so with humble men I may have a sense and feling of humilitie, with devoute men I may sounde out alowde the lauds and praises of God, and continually render thankes to him for his benefits; and then after being aided by the praiers of many, I may runne more safely to the marke which I shoote at, and withoute perill attaine to the price that is promised, as I am not ignorant that the snares and wiles of oure auncient enemies are infinite; for he is the slye serpent, which lieth in the shadow of woods, winding, whirling and turning aboute many waies, and with his wiles and subtile shifts he attempteth maruelously to delude and abuse the soules of the simple which want a faithfull guide; in so much as it is not without cause that we are admonished to *trie the spirits, if they be of God.* To you, therefore, bicause you are spirituall, and accustomed to this kinde of conflict, I commend all this businesse, beseching you even by the boweles of God's mercy that you would vouchsafe to direct me with your counsaile and wisdom. And if in youre sight it seme profitable for more honor to God, more commoditie to his Churche and eternall salvation to my soule, that I be preferred to that Societie of the most holie name of

Jesus; then presently before God and in the court of my conscience I do promise obedience to all and singular Rectors & governours established allredie, or to be hereafter established, & likewise to all rules or lawes received in this societie, to the uttermoste of my power and so farre as God doth give me grace: God is my witnesse, and this my owne hand writting shalbe a testimonie hereof in the day of Iudgement. As for the healthe of my body, you have no cause to doubt, for now well nere I have recovered my former strength and hardnesse, by God's help, and I wax every day stronger than other. Thus in all other things commending my self to your praiers, I bid you farewell in oure Lorde, carefully expecting what you thinke good to determin of me. Vale.

Upon Campion, Sherwine and Brian

WHAT iron hart that wold not melt in greefe?
What steele or stone could kepe him dry from teares,
To see a *Campion* haled like a theefe
to end his life with both his glorious freres,
in whose three deathes unto the standers by
even all the world almost might seeme to dye.

England must lose a soveraigne salve for sinne,
a sweet receit for suttle heresie,
India a saint her seely soules to winne,
Turky a bane for her idolatrie,
the Church a souldier against Babylon,
to batter hell & her confusion.

The skowling skies did storme & puff apace,
they could not bear ye wrongs y^t malice wrought;
The sunn drew in his shining purple face,
the moistened clouds shed brinish tear for thoght;
the river Thames a while astonied stoode,
to count the drops of *Campion's* sacred blood.

Nature with teares bewailed her heavy losse,
Honesty feard her selfe should shortly dye,
Religion saw her Champion on the crosse,
Angels and saints desired leave to cry,
even Heresie the eldest child of Hell
began to blush, & thought she did not well.

And yet, behold, when *Campion* made his end,
his humble hart was so bedewde with grace
that no reproach could once his mind offend,
Mildness possest his sweet & cherefull face
A pacient spectacle was presented then,
in sight of God, of angels, saints & men.

The heavens did cleare, ye sun like gold did shine,
the clouds were dry, the fearful river ranne,
Nature & vertue wypt their watred eyen,
religion joyed to see so mild a man,
men, angels, saints and all that saw him dye
forgot their grief, his joyes appeared so nye.

They saw his patience did expect a crowne,
his scornful cart a glorious heavenly place,
his lowly mind a happy high renowne,
his humble cheare a shining angel's face,
his feare, his griefe, his death & agonie,
a joy, a peace, a life in maiestie.

From thence he prayes & sings in melodie
for our recure, & calleth us to him,
he stands before the throne with harmonie,
and is a glorious suter for our sinne:
With wings of love he jumped up so hye,
to help the cause for which he sought to dye.

Rejoice, be glad, triumph, sing himmes of joye!
Campion, Sherwine, Brian live in bliss;
they sue, they seeke the ease of our annoy,
they pray, they speake, & all effectuall is;
not like to men on earth as heretofore,
but like to saints in heaven, and that is more.

*The Martyrdomes of the Reverend Priestes
M. Thomas Forde, M. John Sherte and M.
Robert Johnson, the xxviij of Maye,
1582. And first of M. Thomas Forde,
Priest and Maister of Arte*

Chap. IV

THEY were all trailed upon herdles from the Tower of London alonge the streates thereof unto Tyborne, betwixt vj & vij of the clocke in the morning. First *M. Forde* being set up in the carte, he blessed himselfe with the signe of the Crosse, being so weake as he fell downe in the carte, and after he was up he said, 'I am a Catholike, and do dye in the Catholike religion,' and therewith he was interrupted by *Sherife Martine* saying, 'You come not hither to confesse your religion, but as a traitor and malefactor to the Queene's Maiestie and the whole Realme, moving and sturing of sedition. And therefore I pray you goe to and confesse your faulte, and submitte yourselfe to the Queene's mercie, and no doubt but she would forgive you.'

Whereunto he answered, 'That supposed offence whereof I was endyted and condemned was the conspiring of her Maiestie's death at Rome and Rhemes, whereof I was altogether not guilty. For the offence was supposed for conspiring the Queene's Maiestie's death in the 22 yere of her

They cannot abid the confession of the Catholike faith

They harpe all waies upon one string that will not sound

Neither was he ever at Rome or Remes in all his life

Maiestie's raigne, at which time I was in England remaining, and long before that, for I have remained here for the space of vj or vij yeres, and never departed this realme; whereof I might bring the witnes of an hundreth, yea fyve hundreth sufficient men. And I had thereupon been discharged at the barre if I would have disclosed their names with whom I had been, which I did forbeare onely for feare to bring them into trouble.'

Then *Sherife Martine* said, 'Here is your own hand writing, with the testimonie of worshipfull men, as the Queene's Attorney, *D. Hammon, D. Lewes* and others. And if that will not serve, here is one of your owne companions that was the Pope's scholler to testifie your offence.' To the which *M. Forde* answered, 'That notwithstanding I am altogether not guilty, whatsoever you have written.'

He continued for the moste parte in praier secretly to himself during the time that the Sherife or any other spake to him. Then was a scrolle of his examination redd by a Minister. To some articles he said nothing, but to others he said that the Pope for some causes may depose a prince of his estate and dignitie and discharge the subiects of their deuties & allegeance, 'For (quoth he) this question was disputed xiiij yeres since at Oxford by the divines there, before the Queene's Maiestie, and there it was made and proved to be a most cleere case in her own presence.'[18]

And here being interrupted, *Munday*, the Pope's scholler, beinge called as a witness, said that *Forde* was privey to their conspiracies, but was not able to affirme that ever he saw him beyond the seas. This his assertion *M. Forde* utterly denied upon his death. And being asked what he thought of the Queene's Maiestie & withal willed to aske her and the whole realme whom he had stirred to sedition, forgive-

---

A notable charitie and worthy such a priest

Nothing will serve to prove their condemnation to be just

Though not determined by whom the prince might be deposed

See Note 18

A notable companion for their purpose: that will beare witnes of that which he never saw nor heard in his life

nes; he said that he acknowledged her for his Sufferaine and Queene, and that never in his life he offended her, & so praying secretly, desired all those that were of his faith to pray with him and ended with this praier, '*Jesus, Jesus, Jesus, esto mihi Jesus,*' and hanged until his fellow *M. Shert* (belike to terrifie him the more) might see him.

Innocencie

Of Mr John Shert Priest
Chap. V

M SHERT being broght from the herdle, and seeing his fellow *M. Forde* hanged before him, with a confident courage, smyling countenance, and with his handes lifted up, he spake as followeth, *O happie Tom. Happie arte thou that didst runne that happie race. O benedicta anima, thou art in good case. Thou blessed soule pray for me.* And being lifted into the carte, he desired all Catholikes to pray for him, and turning to the place of execution (by the commaundement of the Sherife) seeing his fellow boweled and beheaded, he kneeled downe, and cried, *O Tom, O happie Tom, O blessed soule, happie arte thou, thy blessed soule pray for me.* And being found fault withal, because he praied to those that were dead, he said: *O blessed ladie, mother of God, pray for me, and all the Sainctes of heaven pray for me.* The Sherife finding fault with this as with erronius doctrine, he answered that it was booth sound and true doctrine, which he would now seale with his bloud & after beganne as foloweth.

'O blessed Lord, to thee be all honour and praise. First,

His martyrdom & innocencie proved him to be a Sainct, and as to such a on be praied

They cannot abid our Lady to be praied unto neitheer

A marvelous constancy

I give thee most hartie thankes, for that thou didst create me of nothing, to thy likenes and similitude. Secondly, for my redemption by the death of thy sweete sonne Jesus Christ my Saviour and Redeemer. And lastly that thou wilt bring me thy poore servant to so glorious & happie a death for thy sake, although in the eies of the worldlinges contumelious and reprocheful, yet to me most joyful & glorious, and for the which I yeld the most hartie thankes.' And therewith was letted to proced further by the Sherife, who said to him, 'Aske the Queene forgivenes for these treasons, whereof thou arte condemned.' Who answered, 'The asking of forgivenes doth implie an offence done, for me to charge myself being innocent, it were not my deutie. We have been racked and tormented for these things, and nothing hath been found. Also we have been twice examined since our condemnation, which hath not been seen heretofore in any malefactor. Those supposed treasons, whereof I am condemned, I leave betweene God and myselfe, and upon my death I am altogether innocent and faultless. I utterly refuse to aske her forgivenes for this fact whereof I am condemned, for that I am not guilty: but if in any other privat matter I have offended, I aske her and all the world forgivenes. It is impossible for me to be guilty of the conspirace at Rhemes or Rome, being in England long time before the said supposed treasons committed, and continuing here stil sithence.' The which *Munday* being his accuser did not much denie, for he said he never knew him beyond the seas neither at Rome nor at Rhemes.

Then Sherife Martine requested a minister that stood besyde to reade the examination. Who answered, 'As the man is obstinate now, so upon his examination was he as obstinate, for he uttered nothing that is to be red.' But

Marginalia:
A goodly speech worthie such a Martyr

They seeme in the eies of fooles to die. Sap. 3

M. Sherife loveth not such good talke

Douting themselves of the uniust condemnation, were forced to seeke new matter

A prety trick

that notwithstanding he red the preface of the booke, containinge as is there to be seen. Which being redd, the Sherife desired *M. Sherte* again to knowledge his offence, seeing that it was so manifest, and to aske the queene forgivenes; affirming that the queene would deale very mercifully with him, and that he had authoritie himself if he did acknowledge his fault, to stay his execution, and to returne him backe without more adoe. And as even not long since I found fault with you for swearing & you cryed God mercie therefor, so now here confesse your offences and be sorie for them. Who answered, 'Should I for saving this carkas condemne my soule? God forbid.' Being asked what he thought of the Queene's Maiestie, answered: 'I acknowledge her for my soveraigne ladie and queene, for whose prosperous estat and well doing, in prison and at libertie, I did alwaies pray.' And being demaunded whether he thought her to be supreme governor under Christ of the Church of England? he said:

'I wil geve to *Cæsar* that which is his & to God that that belongeth to God. *She is not, nor cannot be; nor any other, but only the supreame pastor.*' 'What, do you meane, that whore of Babilon the Pope?' said the Sherife, 'Take heed, M. Sherife, (quoth *M. Sherte*) for the day will come when that shall be a sore word for your soule, & then it shall repent you that ever you called Christe's vicar-general in earth, *whoore*. When you and I shal stand at one barre, before that indifferent iudge, who iudgeth all things aright; then, I say, will you repent your saying. Then must I geve testimonie against you.' And the hangman making readie at the importunate clamour of the people, who cried to dispatch, saying, that he had lived too long, he delivered his handkercheefe to the hangman with two shillings therein,

It was manifest by the preface of their owne making what a mockery is this

'They knew that he was as innocent as the Q merciful.' A markable saying

Innocencie

When they can find no temporal and old treasons they flee to the spiritual treasons of their owne making

A worthie admonition

As the Iewes cried against Christ & S. Steven at the instigation of the Pharesies, so now moved by the Ministers

saying, 'Take this for thy hire, & I pray God forgeve thee,' leaving this warning and testimonie to the whole people in a loud voice, that al might here him, denouncing as foloweth:

'*Whosoever dieth out of the Catholique Church he dieth in the state of damnation.*' Therewith, turned almost rounde about, held up his hands wagging them to the people, and then beganne to pray as followeth: '*Domine Jesu Christe, fili Dei vivi, pone passionem, crucem et mortem tuam, inter judicium tuum et animas nostras,*'[19] etc., with his *Pater Noster, Ave Maria*, and other like praiers. And when the carte was trailed away, his hands being before on high, in the putting them downe, he light upon the rope, and so held it and the officers pulled them downe. The Sherife then said, 'Notwithstanding his obstinacie, see how willing he is to live.' So he hanged till he was dead, but it semed to me that his hands by chance, as he was putting them downe, fell upon the rope which he by chance held fast in his hands, as (in that case) he would have done any other thing if he had chanced upon it.

marginalia: England can have no excuse, being so notoriously warned.

Have not Catholikes cofidence in Christ's passion?

See Note 19

A malicious and folish interpretation, for a man dying, naturally, taketh hold of anything he lighteth on

M. Robert Johnson, Priest

Chap. VI

M. JOHNSON being brought from the herdel, was commaunded to look upon *M. Sherte* who was hanging, and then immediately cut downe. And so being holpen into the carte, was commaunded againe to look backe towards *M. Sherte* who was then in quartering. And after he turned him, and signed himselfe with the signe of the crosse,

marginalia: A new inhumane practis, to terrifie them, and to force them by horror to confesse the things wherof they were innocent

OF FATHER EDMUND CAMPION 63

saying, *In nomine Patris, et Filij et Spiritus sancti.* 'Dispatch, quoth the sherife, & speake quietly.' 'I would be sorie,' answered M. *Johnson,* 'to trouble or offend your worship.' 'You shall not offend me,' saith the Sherife, 'so that you offend not God.'

Johnson. 'I am a Catholike, and am condemned for conspiring the Queene's Maiestie's death at Remes, with the other companie who were condemned with me. I protest, that as for some of them, with whom I was condemned to have conspired withall, I did never see them before we met at the barre, neither did I ever write unto them, or receive letters from them, and as for any treasons I am neither guiltie in deede nor thought.'

Sherife. 'Your owne hand subscribed to your examination taken by men of good consciences, the servants of God, M. *Poppam* atturney general, M. *Egerton* the solicitor, M. *Lewes* and M. *Hammon* doctors of the civil law, shall be laid against you. Also if that will not serve, you shall have him who was the Pope's scholler & a companion amongst you to testifie your treasons *viva voce,* one *Munday.*'

Whereupon M. *Johnson's* examination, now in print, was red, his answers to the vj articles proposed are as above. But they urged him further touching the fifth and the sixth articles. And the Minister redd his answer to the fifth article to be, that he allowed of *Saunders* & *Bristowe's* doings and writings. To the which he answered and said, 'My answere was not so as you read it (neither in truth was it so in the booke) but I answered, and so I say now, that as for the doings of D. *Saunders* and D. *Bristowe* I am altogether ignorant of, neither was I ever privy to their factes, and how then could I approve or disalow them? This was my answere then, and now also I say the same.' To the last

Crosses trouble them. The mildnes of the martyr

Plaine innocencie

God make them his servants, for divers of them do against their conscience

When all faileth Munday is ready to helpe at a pinch with his othe & testimonie

These Ministers can do nothing sincerely

He was not condemned for this treason

article his answer was red, and now beinge demaunded of the same, he said he was of the same minde still and would die in the same minde.

Sherife. 'Well, that is high treason. But you shall heare also what your owne companion, named *Munday*, can say against you.' Whereupon *Munday* was called and came nigh to the carte.

Johnson. '*Munday*, did thou ever knowe me beyond the seas, or was I ever in thy company?'

Munday. 'I was never in your company, neither did I ever know you beyond the seas. But I was privy to your most horrible treasons, whereof you was most clerely convicted, I speake this with safe conscience. And were not priestes sent from Avinion for that purpose? I pray God you may repent you thereof, and that you may die a good subject.'

Johnson. '*Munday*, God geve thee grace to repent thee of thy deedes; truly thou art a shrewd fellow; but there is no time now to reason these matters with thee, only I protest before God, I am not guiltie of any treason.'

Sherife. 'Dost thou acknowledge the Queene for lawful Queene? Repent thee, and notwithstanding thy traitorous practices, we have authoritie from the Queene to carrie thee backe.'

Johnson. 'I do acknowledge her as lawful as Queene Marie was. I can say no more, but pray to God to geve her grace, and that she may now stay her hand from shedding of innocent bloude.'

Sherife. 'Dost thou acknowledge her supreme head of the Church in ecclesiastical matters?'

Johnson. 'I do acknowledge her to have as full and great authority as ever *Queene Marie* had; and more with saftie

---

He is indeed a companion but never his companion

Munday's conscience may be turned into a proverbe

A most impudent and folish lie

How gladly they would have them to confess that which never was to save their credites for murdering of the rest

A necessarie admonition

They flee to matters of religion

of conscience I can not geve her.' The Sherife & other said, 'Thou art a traitor most obstinat.'

Johnson. 'If I be a traitor for maintaining this faith, then was *King Henry*, and all the kinges and queenes of this realme before time, and all our auncitours traitors, for they mainteined the same.' *How prove you that?*

Sherife. 'What? You will preach treason also, if we suffer you?'

Johnson. 'I teach but the Catholike Religion.'

One demaunded, 'What do you meane by Catholike Religion?'

Johnson. 'I meane that religion whereof the Pope is supreme pastor.' Then a minister asked him, 'What, was Athanasius a Catholike? What held he?' To whom *M. Johnson* answered, 'I am not so well red in Athanasius to know all his opinions.' The other said, 'I am shure you have read *Quicunque vult*, etc.' Whereunto *M. Johnson* gave no great attention, but he said againe, 'What? have you not redd Athanasius creede *Quicunque vult*, etc.?' 'Yes, said he, that I have, and I believe it to be good and Catholike.' But in all that, said the Minister, you can not find the Pope once named.' 'It is not necessary (quoth *M. Johnson*), the Pope should be named in everything that appertaineth to the Catholike Faith.' *An argument meet for a Minister*

Whereupon the rope was put about his necke, and he was willed to pray, which he did in latin. They willed him to pray in English that they might witnes with him. He said, 'I pray that praier which Christ taught in a tongue I well understand.' *But God doeth to whom he praied, neither needeth he any witnes thereof*

Sherife. 'But we do not understand it.'

Johnson. 'I do thinke your Worship doth understand it.'

Sherife. 'If I do, others do not. Wherefore pray in English that others may testifie it and pray with you.'

An other Minister cried, 'Pray as Christ taught.'

Johnson. 'What, do you think that Christ taught in English?'

M. Johnson praied in latin, saying his *Pater Noster* his *Ave* and *Creede* and *In manus tuas*, etc., & so the carte was trailed away, and he finished this life as the rest did. All hanged until they were dead, and so cut downe and quartered.

The Ministers speaches are e'ver like themselves

*The Martyrdomes of the Reverend Priests
M. William Filbie, M. Lucas Kirbie, M. Laurence Richardson, whose right name was
Johnson, and M. Thomas Cottam the 30th
May, 1582. And first of M. William Filbie, native of Oxford*

Chap. VII

ON Wednesday being the 30 of May these four venerable Priests above named were trailed from the Tower of London along the streates to Tyborne, about vij of the clocke in the morning. When they were come to the place of execution, *William Filbie* (being the youngest, not above xxvij yeres of age) was first taken from the herdle, and being lifted into the carte, he blessed himself with the signe of the Crosse, saying, *In nomine Patris & Filii & Spiritus sancti* and so proceded with these wordes: 'Let me see my brethren,' looking to the other which lay on the herdle, & therewithal holding forthe his handes to them, said, 'Pray for me.' Then speaking to the companie, said: 'I am a Catholike, and I protest before almightie God that I am innocent of all these matters, whereof I am condemned, and I hope to be saved by the merits and death of our Saviour Jesus Christ; beseeching him to have mercie on me and to forgive me my offences.'

And therewithal a proclamation was red for keeping the Peace, and at the end thereof was said, *God save the Queene.* To which he said, *Amen.*

Innocencie

The people asking him for what Queene he praied for, he answered, 'For Queene Elizabeth, beseeching God to send her a long & quiet raigne, to his good will, and make her his servant, and preserve her from her enimies.' With that *M. Topcliff* and others willed him to say, 'God save her from the Pope.' To whom he answered, 'He is not her enemie.' Therewith the Minister of S. Andrewes in Holborne said,

A Minister's note

'Note, that he saith the Pope is not the Queene's enemie.' And then a preacher called *Charke*, 'Yes, said he, you are a traitor, for you are sworne to the Queene's sworne enemie.' *M. Filbie* looking aside, said, 'What do you meane? I never toke othe in all my life.' 'What, said *Charke*, then are you not a Priest?' 'You are deceived, said *M. Filbie*, it is a vow and not an othe.' After that one of

A promise of obedience to his ordinarie: but therein no mention of the Pope

the Sherife's men standing in the carte with *M. Filbie*, said unto him, 'What hast thou there in thy handkerchefe?' And therewithal taking the handkerchiefe from him found a little Crosse of wodde within it, which he holding up in his handes said, *O what a villanous traitor is this, that hath a Crosse,* divers times repeating it, and divers of the people saying the same. Whereunto *M. Filbie* answered nothing, onely smiling at them.

He was no more ashamed of this his Saviour's banner than of his crown, the which he made shift to shave

Then the articles, with the preface of the booke printed by authoritie was redd, and his answers unto them. It was replied against him by some urging him further upon the same answer: 'If you hold this, then you can not be but a traitor to the Queene's Maiestie, for that the Pope hath deposed her by his Bull.' *M. Filbie* said, that that Bull was perchance called in again by this *Pope Gregorie* the 13.

To the sixt article he answered, that if he had been in Irland, he would have done as a Priest should have done, that is to pray that the right might take place. To whom some replied, 'Did *Saunders* well in that fact of Irland?' 'I know not, quoth he, I was not privie to his doinges. I never saw him or spake with him. Let him answer for himself.'

Then *Sherife Martine* called upon the hangman to dispatch, and the roope being about his necke, the Sherife said, '*Filbie*, the Queene is merciful unto you, and we have authoritie from her to carie you backe, if you will aske her mercie, and confesse your fault. Doe not refuse mercie offered, aske the Queene's forgivenes.' To whom *M. Filbie* answered, 'I never offended her.' ' Well then, said the Sherife, make an ende.' And thus desiring all Catholikes to pray for him he praied, saying his *Pater Noster*, his *Ave*, & *In manus tuas*, etc., and when the carte was trailing away he said, *Lord, receive my soul*, and so hanged knocking his breast several times, till some pulled down his handes, and so finished his life.

Innocencie

Of M. Luke Kirbie, Priest
and *M. of Arte*

Chap. VIII

THEN was *M. Luke Kirbie* brought to see his fellow hang, and being lifted up to the carte, he beganne thus: '*O my frendes, O my frendes*, I am come hither for supposed treason, although in deede it be for my conscience,' and after praied thus, ' *O my Saviour Jesus Christ*, by whose death and passion I hope to be saved, forgive me sinfull sinner, my manifold sinnes and offences, etc.,' and being commaunded to torne towardes the place of execution, his fellow *M. Filbie* being beheaded, and as the manner is, the executioner lifting his head between his handes, he cried, 'God save the Queene,' to the which *M. Kirbie* said, 'Amen,' & being asked 'What Queene?' he answered 'Queene Elizabeth,' to whom he praied God to send a long and prosperouse raigne, and preserve her from her enemies. *Charke* willed him to say 'from the Pope, his curse and power.'

Kirbie. 'If the Pope leavie warre against her, or curse her uniustly, God preserve her from him also; and so to direct her in this life as that she may further & mainteine Christ's Catholike Religion, & at last enherite the kingdom of heaven.'

And after, he made a solemne protestation of his innocencie in that whereof he was condemned, adding that if there were any living that could iustly accuse him in any one point of that whereof he was condemned, he was ready to submitte himself to her Maiestie's clemencie. And seeing *Munday* present, he desired he might be brought in, to say what he could. Who being brought in, said that being at Rome he persuaded him & another yong man named *Robinson* to stay there, and not to come to England, for that shortly some stirre or trouble was like to come. And seeing that could not stay him, he said that he willed him to persuade those that were his frendes to the Catholike religion againe the great day. To which *M. Kirbie* answered that it was unlike that he, who knew him before his departure from Rome, how he was affected in religion, would utter any such wordes to him, to persuade the people. To which *Munday* replied that it was like, because he delivered

An undiscrete question putting a scruple into the people's heades

him some hallowed pictures to carie with him. To the which *M. Kirbie* answered that because he mistrusted him he would not deliver, nor did deliver him any. But he said he did deliver him two Julies to bie pictures. And that now he was very ingratfully dealt withal, being by him falsely accused: he being such a benefactor to all his contreimen, although he knew them to be otherwise affected in religion than himself was. For he said he spake to some of the Pope's chieffest officers, and was like through them to come to trouble. To others he said he delivered the shert off his backe, and travailed with others fortie miles for their saffe conduct, and onely for good will. And said further that unwitting to *Munday* he wrot a letter to one in Remes to deliver him fiften shillinges, which he never received, because he never went to receive it.

And he urged *Munday* againe in the feare and love of God to say but the truth, alledging farther how *Nicolls*, who in his bookes uttered much more of him than *Munday* did, yet his conscience accusing him, he came to his chamber in the Tower and in presence of foure, whereof he named his keeper to be one, recanted and denied that which before he had affirmed in his bookes. One *Topcliffe* said, 'How do you know that *Nicolls* hath recanted?' *M. Kirbie* answered, 'He came into my chamber in the Tower, and there before foure he said these words.' (*See M. Kirbie's letter at the ende of this tragedie.*)

Then the Sherife interrupted him and said: 'Even as he hath recanted his error, and is sorie for it, so do you.' *M. Kirbie* not regarding his wordes passed on, and shewed likewise that this *Munday* in presence of *Sir Owen Hopton* and others did say that he could charge him with nothing. Which *Munday* denied. But he affirmed it againe, and said

Then he accused him falsely and so there is no cause why he should confesse it

that then one that was present said that upon that confession he might take advantage. Then the Sherife asked who that was, and he after a while answered that it was one *Coudridg*.[20]

See Note 20

After this his answer to the forsaid articles was redd: where to the first, bein examined, he said that the excommunication of *Pius Quintus* was a matter of fact, wherein the Pope might erre, 'the which I do leave to himself to answer for.' And where he said that the Pope for some causes might depose a prince, now he did explaine it, that it was a question disputable in scholles whether the Pope might depose princes. And being asked by *Topcliff* whether he would die for a matter disputable in scholles, he said he did only yeld his opinion.

To the second, he added further, that he thought some of the lerned that were there present would affirme that also. Whereat divers with on voice said, 'No.' Whereupon *M. Kirbie* called for one *M. Crowley* once or twise. And a Minister brought a place out of Salomon, which saith, '*By me Kinges rule and Tyrants are exalted*'; and an other out of the Gospel where it is said unto Pilat, '*Thou shouldest not have any power against me unles it were geven the from above.*' Proving that because their authoritie was from God no one might have authoritie to displace them. And one Minister there argued thus to the same poorpose, that every soule must be subiect to superior powers, 'and therefore, quoth he, the Pope himselfe if he be a soule must be subiect and consequently cannot depose others of their soveranitie.' And *M. Kirbie* being about to answer, was interrupted by an other Minister, who alleged the practise of the primitive Church, when notwithstanding that Christians lived under heathen princes, yet they did obey them. To which

By this Minister's argument the Emperor could not have deposed Pilat from his presidentshipe

As though the Queene were not a soule also, and the Pope in higher superioritie than she

M. *Kirbie* said that the case did differ, for where the Prince is once a Christian and after falleth to infidelitie, there he may be disobeied, but where he was never Christian the case is otherwise. To the fourth, answering as befor, 'Notwithstanding, saith he, I acknowledge to my Prince and Quene as much deutie and authoritie as ever I did to Quene Marie, or as any subiect in France, Spain or Italie, do acknowledge to his King or prince. And more I cannot nor ought not of deutie give her.' And thereupon *Topcliff* demaunded, 'What if all they be traitors, will you be a traitor too?' To which he answered, 'What, be they all traitors? God forbid, for if all they be traitors then all our auncestors have been traitors likewise. And as for *D.D. Saunders* and *Bristow* they might erre in their private opinions, the which I will defend no further then they doe agree with the iudgement of Christ's Catholike Church.'

Being demaunded whether he thought the Queene to be supreme governesse of the Church of England, he answered he was redy to yeld her as much authoritie as any other subiect ought to yeld his prince, or as he would yeld to Queene Marie, and more with saftie of conscience he could not do. Then *Sherife Martine* tould him that the Queene was merciful and would take him to her mercie, so he would confesse his deutie towards her, and forsake *that man of Rome*, and that he had authoritie himselfe to stay execution and carie him backe againe.

Who answered that to deny the Pope's authoritie was a point of faith which he would not deny for saving of his life, beinge sure to damne his soule. Then was it tendered him that if he would but confesse his fault and aske the Queene forgevenes she would yet be merciful to him. He answered againe that his conscience did give him a cleere

The Church has no authority over infidels: but over all Christians

Wisely

O marvelous constancie

testimonie that he never offended, and therefore he would neither confesse that whereof he was innocent, neither aske forgevenes, where no offence was committed against her Maiestie.

By these numbers of proffers, it is plaine they iudged them innocent in their conscience

'Well, then, said *Sherife Martine,* doe but acknowledge those thinges which your fellow *Bosgrave* hath done, such as appereth by his examination and I will yet save your life.' Who denied likewise.

Then the people cried, 'Away with him,' and he beganne to pray in Latin; the Ministers and others desired him to pray in English and they would pray with him, who answered that in praying with them he should dishonor God, 'But if you were of one faith with me, then I would pray with you.' But he desired all those that were Catholikes to pray with him and he would pray with them; and as for any other that was a Christian and desirous to pray for him, he would not let them, although he would not pray with them. And so, after that he had ended his *Pater Noster* and began his *Ave,* the carte was drawen away and there he hanged until he was dead, and until his two fellowes *Richardson* and *Cottam* did take the vewe of him. His speaches were very intricat for that many did speake unto him & of several matters, but here are the principal thinges by him uttered to my remembrance:

¶ *A true copy of a letter sent by that constant confessor, Maistre Kirby, to certaine his friendes*

MY moste hartie commendations to you and the rest of my derest frendes. If you sende anything to me you must make hast, because we look to suffer death very shortly, as alreadie it is signified to us. Yet I much feare lest our unworthines of that excellent perfection and crowne of martyrdome shall procure us a longer life. Within these fewe daies *John Nicholls* came to my chamber windowe, with humble submission to crave mercy and pardon for all his wickednes and trecheries committed against us, and to acknowledge his bookes, sermons and infamous speaches to our infamy and discredit, to be wicked, false and most execrable before God and man, which for preferment, promotion, hope of livinge, and favor of the nobilitie, he committed to writing, and to the vewe of the worlde, whereof beinge verye penitent and sorrowfull from his hart, rather then he would commit the like offence againe, he wisheth to suffer a thousand deaths. For being pricked in conscience with our uniust condemnation, which now hath happened contrarie to his expectation, albeit he offered matter sufficient in his first booke of recantation for our adversaries to make a bill of endightement against us, yet he minded then nothinge lesse, as he now protesteth. He knoweth in conscience our accusations, and evidence brought in against us to be false, and to have no coullor of truth, but onelie of malice forced by our ennimies. And for *Sledd* and *Mundaye*, he is himself to accuse them of this wicked treacherie and falshoode, and of their naughtie and abominable life, of which he was made privie, and which for shame I can not committ to writinge. In detestation of his owne doinges and their wickednes, he is minded never hereafter to ascend into pulpet, nor to deale againe in any matter of religion, for which cause he hath forsaken the Ministerie, and is minded to teach a schole (as I understande by him) in Norfolke, in profe whereof he shewed me his new disguised apparell, as yet covered with his Minister's weede. I wished hym to make amendes for all his sinnes, and to go to place of pennance, and he answered me, he was not yet conformable to us in every point of religion, nor ever was, but lived in Rome in hipocrisie, as he hath done ever since in his owne profession. Againe, he thought, that if ever he should departe the realme, he coulde not escape burning.

He offered to go to Maister Lieutenant, and to Maister Secretaire *Walzingham*, and to declare how iniuriously I and the rest weare condemned, that he himself might be free from sheddinge Innocent bloude, albeit he was somewhat affraid to shew himself in London, where alreadie he had declared our innocent behaviour, and his owne malitious dealinge towardes us in his booke and sermons.

To give my censure and Iudgement of him, certain I thinke that he will within short time fall into infidelitie except God of his goodnes in the meane time be mercifull unto him, and reclaime him by some good means to the Catholike faith; yet it should seeme he hath not lost all good gifts of nature, when as in conscience he was pricked to open the truth in our defence, and to detect his owne wickednes and trecheries of others, practised against us to our confusion.

Now I see, as all the world herafter shall easilie perceave, that the doinges of this man do confirme the old saying: That rather then God will have wilful murther to be concealed, he procureth the birdes of the aier to reveale it.

I am minded to signifie to *Sir Francis Walzingham* this his submission unto us, except in the meane time I shall learne that he hath (as promised faithfully to me) alreadie opened the same. *Maister Richardson* and *Maister Philbie* have now obtained some bedding, which ever since their condemnation have laine upon the bordes. *Maister Hart* had many and great conflictes with his adversaries. This morning, the x of Januarie, he was committed to the dongeon, where he now remaineth. God comfort him. He taketh it verie quietlie & patiently; the cause was for that he would not yeld to *Maister Reignoldes* of Oxford, in any one point, but still remained constant the same man he was before and ever. *Maister Reignoldes*, albeit he be the best learned of that sort, that hath from time to time come hither to preach and conferre, yet the more he is tried and dealt with all the lesse learning he hath shewed. Thus beseeching you to assist us with your good praiers, whereof now especially we stande in neede, as we by God's grace shall not be unmindefull of you. I bid you farewell, this x of Januarie, 1582.

Yours to death and after death,
LUKE KIRBIE

Of M. Laurence Richardson, whose right name was Johnson, and M. Thomas Cottam, Priests and Graduates

Chap. IX

THESE two were brought together to looke upon *M. Kirbie*, which was then hanging, and being cut downe, they were put up into the carte, where with cheerefull countenances they signed themselves with the signe of the Crosse, saying, *In nomine Patris & Filij & Spiritus sancti.* M. *Cottam* turning him about said, *God blesse you all. Our Lord blesse you all*: with a smiling countenance. M. *Richardson* being commaunded by the sherife's man to look upon his fellow, who was in cutting up said: *O God's will be done.*

Here he blesseth the people, and never cursed them, as lying Munday writeth in his Discoverie of Ed. Campion

With that, one *Field* a preacher said, 'Dispatch, dispatch.' To whom *M. Cottam* said with smiling countenance, 'What are you an executioner or a preacher? Fye, fye.' A minister standing by said, 'Leave off those iestes, it is no time to ieste. He is a preacher, not an executioner, he commeth to exhorte you to die well.'

Cottam. 'Truly by his wordes he seemed to be an executioner, for he said, Dispatch, dispatch.'

Field. 'I did not say these wordes to any such entent, but that they which were about the other should be quiet.'

Cottam. 'I crie God mercie for all my idle wordes, and I beseech you M. Sherife, that you will not be offended with me, for truly I would lye under your horse feete to be troden upon befor I should offend you.'

Then *M. Richardson* being placed right under the place where he should hang, divers moved speaches to him all at one time. To whom he answered, 'I pray you do not trouble me. If you demaund any questions of me, let them be touching the matter whereof I was condemned, and do not move new questions.' And thereupon he was turned backe to look upon *M. Kirbie*, who was then in quartering, which he did, and the head being cut off, they held it up, saying, *God save the Queene*, & he being demaunded what he said. 'I say *Amen, I pray God save her*.' And further said: 'I am come hither to die for treason; and I protest before God I am not guilty in any treason more then all Catholike bishops that ever were in this land sithence the conversion thereof till our time, & as well (if they were alyve) might they be executed for treason, as I am now.' To whom a minister replied thus: 'The case is not like, for then Popish priests lived under Popish princes, and did not disobey them, & so were no traitors.'

OF FATHER EDMUND CAMPION

In the meane time many wordes and sentences were uttered by *M. Cottam*. And a Minister amongest other thinges, willed him to confesse his wicked and leude behaviour which he had committed in Fish-streat about foure yeres since.

Cottam. 'What do you meane?'

Sherife. 'He would have you to confesse the filthe you committed in Fish-streat.'

Cottam. 'O blessed Jesus, Thy name be praised. Is this now laid here to my charge?' *A divilish sclaunder raised by the Minister to disgrace the man of God*

The Minister said, 'We do not charge you with it, but we would have you to discharge you thereof if there be any such thing.' *He is charged with this act as truly as with treason*

Another Minister answered, 'No, it was not he, but his brother.'

Cottam. 'You shall hear. You accuse me for filthe committed about four yeres since in Fish-streat, and I was not in London this seven yeres, and if I had done any such thinge, what do you meane to lay it to my charge?' With that ij or iij of them said that it was not he but his brother.

After that whilest they were talking with *M. Richardson*, *M. Cottam* toke *Bull* the hangman by the sleve and said to him, 'God forgive thee and make thee his servant. Take heed in time and call for grace, and no dout God will heare thee. Take example by the executioner of *S. Paul*, who during the time of his execution, a little drope of blood falling from *S. Paul* upon his garment, white like milke, did afterward call him to remembrance of himselfe, and so became penitent for his sinnes, and became a good man; whose example I pray God thou maiest follow, and I pray God give thee of His grace.' *A very zealous & charitable act*

THE DEATH & MARTYRDOM

The wrangeling of a Minister

The Minister of S. Andrew's said, 'What, did milke fall from his breast?'

Cottam. 'No, blood fell from his necke or head, in likenes of milke.'

Minister of S. And. 'What, do you say he was saved by that blood which fell upon him?'

Cottam. 'No, I marvel what you meane,' and so was interrupted by some others to proceade.

Then the articles were redd and his answers to them, adding that as touching the doctrine of *D.D. Saunders* and *Bristow* he alloweth of it so farre forth as they agree with the true Catholike Church of Rome. *Topcliff* and some other ministers said he builded his faith upon *Saunders*. To whom he answered 'I build not my faith upon any one man whatsoever but upon the whole Catholike Church.'

Then the rope being put about both their neckes and fastened to the post, the Sherife said, 'Now, *Richardson*, if thou wilt confesse thy faultes and renounce the Pope, the Queene will extend her mercie towardes thee, and thou shalt be carried backe again.' *M. Richardson* answered, 'I thancke her maiestie for her mercie, but I must not confesse an untruth or renounce my faith.' All this while *M. Cottam* was in praier, and uttering of divers good sentences, saying, 'All that we here sustaine is for saving of our soules,' and therewithal lifting up his eyes to heaven, said: *O Lord, thou knowest our innocencie.* Then he was willed to confesse his treasons. 'O Lord, (said he) how willingly would I confesse if I did know anything that did charg me, and if we had been guilty of any such thing, surely one or other of us either by racking or death, would have confessed it, or els we had been such people as never were hard of. And I protest befor God that before my comming into England, I was

A most notorious evidence of all the innocencie

In the most barborouse place whereof he had found

OF FATHER EDMUND CAMPION   81

armed to go into India; and if I might be sett at libertie, I would never rest but on the iorney to that countrie.' With that the Sherife said, 'The Queene wilbe merciful to thee, if thou wilt thy selfe.' He answered, 'I thancke her grace, saying farther, Do with me what you thinke good.' And therewithal the Sherife commanded that the roope should be losed from the post, and he removed downe from the carte.

Then *M. Richardson* was willed once againe to confesse and aske pardon of the Queene: he answered, that he never offended her to his knowledg. Then *Topcliff* said, 'The like mercie was never shewed to any offender, and if you were in any other common wealth, you should be torne in peces with horses.' Then he was willed to pray. He praied desiring all Catholikes to pray with him. He said his *Pater Noster*, his *Ave*, and his Creede, and when the carte passed, *Lord, receive my soule, Lord Jesus, receive my soule.* And even as the carte passed away *M. Cottam* said, 'O good Lawrence, pray for me. Lord Jesus, receive thy soule,' which he repeated several times. All this time *M. Cottam* was with the Sherife and the rest of the Ministers upon the ground, having the rope still about his necke. I could not well heare what persuasions the Sherife and the Ministers had with him, but I doe coniecture that if he would renounce his faith, he should have his pardon. For I hard him well utter these wordes: 'I will not swarve a iote from my faith, for any thing. Yea, if I had ten thousand lives I would rather lose them all, then forsake the Catholike Faith in any pointe.' And with that he was lifted up into the carte againe. And the Sherife said withal, 'Dispatch him since he is so stubborne.'

Then he was turned backward to looke upon *M. Richardson* who was then in quartering, which he did, saying,

---

better intertainement then here at home

How gladly they would have had anyone of them to confesse the pretended fault

That were strange

A notable constancie

THE DEATH & MARTYRDOM

Innocencie

By this it is evident that all was for religion and not at all for treason

'*Lord Jesus, have mercie upon them: Lord, have mercie upon them. O Lord, give me grace to endure to the end. Lord, give me constancie to the end.*' Which saying he uttered almost for all the time that *M. Richardson* was in quartering, saving once he said, '*Thy soule pray for me.*' And at the last he said, '*O Lord, what spectacle hast thou made unto me?*' the which he repeated twise or thrise, and then the head of *M. Richardson* was holden up by the executioner, who said (as the manner is) *God save the Queene*, to which *M. Cottam* said, 'I beseech God to save her and bless her and with all my hart I wish her prosperity as my lieage and soveraine Queene & cheefe governesse.' They willed him to say 'and supreme head in matters ecclesiastical.' To whom he answered, 'If I would have put in those wordes, I had been discharged almost two years since.' Then the Sherife said, 'You are a traitor if you deny that.' *M. Cottam* said, 'No: that is a matter of faith, and unles it be for my conscience and faith I never offended her maiestie.' And with that he looked up to heaven, and praied secretly and uttered these words, '*In te domine speravi, non confundar in eternum. O domine, tu plura pro me passus es, etc.*,' twice repeating *plura*.

Then the Sherife said to him, 'Yet *Cottam* call for mercie and confesse, and no dout the queene will be merciful unto you.' Who answered 'My conscience giveth me a clear testimonie, that I never offended her': to whom he wished as much good as to his owne soule, whose estat he so favoured and honored, that for all the gold under the cope of heaven he would not wish that any one haire of her head should perish to do her harme. And that all that here he did suffer was for saving his soule, desiring almightie God for his sweete Sonne's sake, that he would vouchsaffe to take him to his mercie, saying that him onely he had offended. Desiring God, that if there were any more unspoken, which were convenient to be spoken, that he would put it into his minde now. And then he praied, desiring all the whole world of forgiveness, and that he did from the bottom of his hart forgive all. Adding that the sinnes of this realme hath deserved infinite punishment and God's iust indignation: desiring him of his mercie, that he would turne his wrath from them, and call them to repentance to see and acknowledge their sinnes. And desiring all Catholikes to pray with him, after he had said his *Pater noster*, and in his *Ave* the carte was driven away, and so hanged till he was dead: and being stripped naked as he hanged, within his sherte he did wear a shert without sleves of very course canvas down beneath his midle. Which belike was a sherte of haire, for the punishment of his body: wherewith England is not now acquainted.

A warning that the sheading of innocent bloud crieth veangeance against the realme

The maner of the Apprehension of Thomas Cottam

AND because the order and maner of M. *Cottam's* first apprehension will cleere him from all suspition of treason and treacherie, and yeld an invincible argument of loyaltie and innocencie, I will set it downe briefly but yet truely, to the great contentation and satisfaction of all good Catholikes, and to the confusion and ignominie of all our bloudie persecutors and adversaries.

The maner and order of his apprehension

Sledd that Notorious varlet, and infamous Iudas (I will not say wickid homicid) having intended to worke some mischefe, came from Rome in the company of divers English men, whose names and markes he toke very diligently; & being come to Lions, found *M. Cottam* there (who having entered into the societie of the name of Jesus at Rome, and being there fallen into a consuming and lingering sicknes, was by his superiors sent to Lions, to trie if by change of aire he might be recovered, but the sicknes so grewe and encreased upon him that he was made an unhable and unfitte man for them, and thereupon they dismissed him) and travailing in his company for some daies iournies, understood of him belike that he ment very shortly to repair home to his native country. Whereupon *Sledd* tooke his markes more exactly and precisely, and being arrived at Paris, there he presented the Lord Embassador with the names and markes he had taken. Who sent them over to the Queene's Counsel, and from them they were sent to the searchers of the portes.

M. Cottam soon after his arrival at Rhemes, being a Deacon and a good preacher long before, was made Priest, and hearing of company that were ready to goe into England, made great hast to goe with them, and ernest shute to have leave, partely for his health, & specially for the great zeal he had to gaine & save soules. He arrived at Dover about the xvj or xviij day of June in the yere 1580, in the company of *M. John Hart* and M. *Edward Rishton* two lerned Priests (which both are also condemned) and an other lay man.

After these iiij had been searched unto their skinnes, and nothing found upon them, and *M. Hart* staid and taken for *M. Orton* (to whom he nothing at all resembled) M. *Cottam* was likewise staid by reason the markes which *Sledd* had given of him, were indeede very cleere and apparent in him. And for the avoiding of charges, one *Allen*, then Maior of Dover, and *Stevens* the searcher requested the lay man M. *Cottam's* companion, who named himself

The cause of M. Cottam's coming out of the Societie and of his retorne to England

M. Cottam staied at the port

Havard,[21] to cary him as a prisoner to my *L. Cobhame*, who agreed very easily thereunto. But as sone as they were out of the towne, 'I can not in conscience, nor will not (quoth *Havard*) being my self a Catholike deliver you a Catholike Priest, prisoner to my *L. Cobham*. But we will straight to London, and when you come there shifte you for your self, as I will do for my self.' Coming to London *M. Cottam* repaired incontinent to one of the prisons and there conferred with a Catholike a friend of his, recounting unto him the order and manner of his apprehension and eskape, his frende told him that, in conscience, he could not make that escape, and perswaded him to goe & yeld himself prisoner. Whereupon he came to his frende *Havard* and requested him to deliver him the Maior of Dover's letter to my *L. Cobham*.

'What will you do with it,' quoth *Havard*. 'Mary,' quoth *Cottam*, 'I will goe and carie it to him, and yeld myself prisoner, for I am fully perswaded that I can not make this eskape in conscience.' 'Why, quoth *Havard*, this councel that hath bene given you procedeth I confesse from a zelous minde. Mary I doute whether it carieth the waight of knowledge with it. You shall not have the letter, nor you may not in conscience yeld yourself to the persecutor and adversarie having so good meanes offered to eskape their crueltie.' But *M. Cottam* persisting still in his demaunde, 'Well, quoth *Havard*, seeing you will not be distorned from this opinion, let us goe first and consult with such a man (naming one but newly cummen then into the realme, whom *M. Cottam* greatly honoured and reverenced for his singular witte and learning, for his rare vertues and other giftes both of body and minde), and if he be of your opinion, you shall have the letter and goe on God's name.'

See Note 21

He was a man of a marvelous zele, and of a timorous conscience

When they came to this man he utterly disliked of his intention, and dissuaded him from so fonnd a cogitation. *M. Cottam* being asswaged but not altogether satisfied, went quietly about his busines, and never voided London for the matter. The Maior of Dover's letter being sente backe unto him again, within ij or iij daies after commeth up the host of the inn where *M. Cottam* was taken.

This host by chance met with *Havard* and taking him by the shulder said, 'Gentilman you had like to have undone me, because the prisoner you promised to deliver is eskaped. Wherefore you must come with me to one *M. Andrewes* my *L. Cobham's* Deputie who lieth at the Starre in New Fish Streat, and give him satisfaction in the matter.' This good fellow *Havard* was somewhat amased at this sodaine sommoning, but after a while being come again to himselfe, saith: 'Why, my host, if I doe deliver you the prisoner againe, you will be contented?' 'Yes,' saith the other, 'deliver me the prisoner, & I have nothing to say to you.' Upon this they went to *M. Cottam's* lodging, but he was removed, the folkes of the house knew not whither. The host would faine have had this *Havard*, so called for the time, to goe with him to the said *Andrewes*, & *Havard* sought all meanes to avoid his company, being sure that, if he had once cumme within the persecutor's pawes, he should not have eskaped them so easily; & being as then loth to fall into further trouble, saith to the other, 'My host, there is no such necessitie why I should goe to *M. Andrewes*, for if I did, peradventure he would pick some quarrel unto me by reason of the prisoner's eskape, & I might come by trouble, & you should reape no gaine or profit thereby. I would be loth therfor to go unto him. But this I will doe for your discharge, I will bring you to a marchant, who I thinke will give you his hand, that I shall bring you the prisoner by iiij of the clocke, or els, that I shall deliver you my body againe.' 'I am content, saith he, so that I have the one of you twoe.' To the marchant they come who, at his brother in law *Havard's* request, gave his hand and promise for the performance of the condition before specified (which promise, albeit it was performed, yet it cost the marchant viii monethes imprisonment afterwards: but how iustly will be one day examined before the iust iudge). This *Havard* leving his host in the marchant's house went furth into the citie with another in his company to see if he could meet with *M. Cottam.*

And coming into Cheapside there by chance he met him, and after ordinary salutations, he said, '*M. Cottam* such a man is come to towne, and hath so seazed upon me for your eskape that you or I must needes goe to prison: you know my state and condition, and may gess how gentely I shall be intreated if I once apeare under my right name before them. Your owne state also you know. Now it is in your choice whether of us shall goe, for one must goe, there is no remedie. And to force you I will not, for I had rather sustaine what punishment soever.' *M. Cottam* lifting up his eies and handes to heaven said these wordes: 'Now God be blessed, I should never while I lived have bene without scruple and grudge of conscience if I had eskaped from them, nothing greveth me, but that I have not dispatched some busines that I have to do.' 'Why, quoth *Havard*, it is but x of the clocke yet, and you may dispatch your busines by iiij of the clocke, and then you may go to them.' 'Whither is it, saith he, that I must go?' 'To the signe of the Starre (quoth *Havard*) in New Fish streat; and there you must enquire for one *M. Andrewes* my *L. Cobham's* deputie. To

A charitable deliberation and most charitable resolution

him you must yeld yourself.' 'I will,' quoth he; and so they departed and never saw one the other after.

This doth prove his innocencie invincibly

And so at iiij of the clocke after he had dispatched all his busines, he went himself all alone to the place appointed, and there yelded himself prisoner, and was carried to the Court lying then at Nonesuch or Otlands, from whence (after five daies conference with divers ministers that laboured, but in vaine, to subvert him) he was sent to the Marshalsee for religion, and not for treason, and from thence to the Tower, there to be racked, not for to reveile any secret treason as the adversaries pretend full falsly, but tormented because he would not confesse his privat sinnes unto them, as he both confidently and truly affirmed to their faces at his arraignment, and so leed to Westminster and there uniustly condemned; and as you have heard, trailed to Tiborne, where he & the rest were cruelly murdered, ending this miserable life by a constant & glorious martyrdom, & now doth follow the immaculat Lambe, to whom be all honnor & glorie for the constancie of these his sainéts. Amen.

*The Order of the Arraignement and Martyr-
dome of M. John Paine, Priest,
2 Aprilis, 1582*

Chap. X

THE 20th of March, 1582, *Sir Owine Hopton,* Lieutenant of the Tower, came to *M. Paine's* chamber dore, and by knocking raised him out of his bed: who had much watched before and provoked him halfe ready to come forth, not telling him to what end: but afterwards advertised how the matter stoode, and perceiving that he was to be removed, he desired leave to retorne into his chamber to make himselfe ready and to fetch his purse, which he had left behinde him, but it would not be graunted, but he commaunded him to be delivered to certaine officers there attending, as he said for his conducting to Essex appointed by the cheefe of the council. *M. Paine* in his cassocke only, went forward with them, being the more gentely dealt with that he was not bound at all.

On Thursday at night his name was recited with about 13 witches, other murderers and theeves. On Friday about 10 of the cloke, he was arraigned after this maner.

First, his endightment was read, viz., that *M. Paine* should utter to *Eliot* at a certaine Christmas lying with

The key of the doore was taken from the keeper and the L. Hopton after her fashion seasea on the purse per usucaptionem

As our Saviour cum iniquis deputatus est, etc.

him in his chamber, that many devises have been heretofore concerning the chang of religion, and yet none have prosperously succeded: but of all others this seemeth the best, 'which I have hearde (quoth he) sometime mentioned of the *Earle of Westmerland, D. Allen,* and *D. Bristowe* that 50 men well appointed with privy coates, and dagges,[22] should espie some opportunitie when the Queene were at progresse, and sley the Queene's Maiestie, the *E. of Leicester* and *M. Walsingham,* and then to proclaime the Queene of Scottes, queene. Also that it should be no greater an offence to kill the Queene then to dispatche a brute beaste.'

This being read, *M. Paine* denied the endightement, and defied all treason. Protesting that he alwaies in minde and worde honored the Queene's Maiestie above any woman in the world, that he would gladly alwaies have spent his life for her pleasure in any lawfull service, that he praied for her, as for his owne soule; that he never invented or compassed any treason against her Maiestie or any of the nobilitie of England.

Then *M. Morice* the Queene's Counseller, on the parte of her Maiestie begane to prove *M. Paine* to be a traitor two waies, by presumption and deposition. The presumption was gathered for that about v yeres past he went beyond the seas and retorned speedely. Secondly, because he was made Priest of the Bishope of Cambray, and so had sworne himselfe to the Pope, who is our most open enemy. Thirdly, that he had speach with traitors in Flaunders, with the *Earle of Westmerland, D. Allen* and *D. Bristowe.* Fourthly, that he travailed with a traitor's sonne, *M. William Tempest.* The deposition was of *Eliot's* othe, and his owne confession on the racke. Consequently *Eliot*

See Note 22

As though the Catholikes would care for these if her M. were dead.

This poore captive ladie is touched in all these forgeries of purpose to make her odious

Either great simplicity or great deceit to say that in taking orders they sweare to the Pope

Persons are named that the lie may seeme more probable

swore that the endightement was true, and *M. Paine's* confession was read.

This being donne, *M. Paine* answered to the presumptions, saying that to goe beyond the seas was not a sufficient token of a traitor, neither to be made Priest of the Bishope of Cambray; for so were many others, nothing at all thinking of treason, confessing also that he was not the Pope's scholler, neither had any maintenance of him. To the third he answered, that he never talked with the *Earle of Westmerland*, and that *D. Allen* and *D. Bristowe* never talked to his knowledge of any such thinges. To the fourth, that *M. Tempest* was an honest gentilman, and never talked with him about treason, neither was it unlawful to keepe him companie, seeing that he was servant to a right honorable counsellor, *Sir Christopher Hatton*.

He refelled *Eliot's* deposition, first, taking God to witnes, on his soule, that he never had such speach with him. Secondly he brought twoe places of Scriptures and a statute to prove that without twoe sufficient witnesses, no man should be condemned; the scriptures are, Iohn 8, v. 17, *The testimonie of two men is true;* and Deut. 17, v. 6, *In the mouth of two or three witnesses shall he perishe, which shall be put to death, let no man be put to death one only bering witnes against him.* Thirdly, he proved *Eliot* insufficient to be a witnes, for oppression of poore men even to death, for a Rape, and other manifest lewde actes with women, for breach of contract, for cozening the *L. Peter* of Money, for changing ofte his religion, for malice against himself, for being attached of murder, and such like actes; after he made a long discourse of *Eliot's* dissembling, when he came to *M. Moore's* for him with a warrant, inducing him to Warwicksheere about his mariage.[23]

When he was at the Seminarie it had no pension of the Pope

1 *Elizab.*6
13 *Elizab.*
1
1 *Ed.* 6, 12

What kinde of men the persecutors procure to be witnesses against God's Priestes

See Note 23

Hereupon a Iury was impanneld, who on friday after dinner brought evidence that he was guilty. Upon Saturday a little befor dinner coming againe to the barre, iudge *Gaudy* asked *M. Paine* what he could say for himselfe. Who answered that he had said sufficiently, alledging that it was against the law of God and man that he should be condemned for one man's witnes, notoriously infamous. Then the iudge said that if he were not guilty the countrey would have found it. *M. Paine* answered, that those men of the Iury were poore, simple men, nothing at all understanding what treason is, and that he had demaunded the definition of conspiracie before of *M. Morice* and them, which they would not give. 'But if it please the Queene and her council that I shall die, I referre my cause to God.' Then the iudge said that his owne wordes made most against him, and if *Eliot* had sworne falsly, his death should be required at his handes, the which no man knewe but God and himselfe. *M. Paine* said that all was but treacherie in seaking of his bloode. In fine iudge *Gaudy* pronounced the sentence of condemnation and afterward exhorted him to repent him selfe, 'Although, said he, you may better instructe me herein.' *M. Paine* demaunded the time when he should suffer, it was answered, on Munday following about 8 of the clocke.

After that he was retorned to prison, the highe Sherife and others came to him and demaunded, Whether he made Jesus Christ the only cause of his salvation. He answered affirmatively, professing unto them the Catholike veritie. All Sunday till v of the clocke, one *D. Withers* and *D. Sone* were with him, persuading him ernestly to chang his religion, 'the which (said they) if you will alter, we doute not to procure mercie for you.' This *M. Paine* tould me

---

A blessed resolution

Neither Eliot's othe, nor the iuries verdit shal excuse the iudge befor God

The people are made beleeve, that Catholikes put not their whole trust in Christ

himselfe, for no body was suffered to come unto them, saying that the Ministers by their foolishe babling did much vexe and trouble him. I amongst many comming unto to him about x of the clocke with the officers, he most comfortably and mekely uttered wordes of constancie unto me and with a loving kisse tooke his leave of me.

Thos men are no fit matter for Ministers to worke on; persons lade with sinne are subiect to their persuasions

The next Morning the ij of April about 8 of the clocke he was laide on the hurdel and brought to the place of execution, where kneeling almost halfe an houre, he earnestly praied, arising and vewing the galloes, he kissed it with a smiling countenance, ascended, and the halter being applied, he lifted up his eies and handes towardes heaven a pretie while, then beganne to speake to the people: first, he made unto them a declaration of his faith (because he was before enformed by me that the common people thought him to be a Iesuit, whose opinion they say is, *That Christ is not God*) confessing one God in essence or substance, and Trinitie in persons, and the Worde to be incarnat for man's redemption, with other Catholike wordes. Secondly, he desired God to forgive him his life past, and to have mercy on all sinners. Thirdly, he forgave all which ever had offended him, naming *Eliot*, whom he desired God most earnestly to make with him a companion in heavenly blisse. Fourthly, he said that his feete did never treade, his handes did never write, nor his witte did never invent any treason against her Maiestie, but he alwaies wished unto her as to his owne soule, desiring almightie God, to give her in earth a prosperouse raigne, and afterwarde eternal felicitie.

By such lying meanes the ministers beguile the people

Wonderful charitie

Innocencie

The *L. Rich* willed him to confesse that he there died a traitor and to be sorry therefore. To whom very paciently he answered that he defied all treason, and to confesse an untruth was to condemne his own soule. 'I confesse truly,

He confessed a trew confession of his innocency before

said he, that I die a Christian Catholike priest.' And desired the *L. Rich* to beare witnes of his death, saying, '*Sweete my Lorde, certify her Maiestie thereof, that she suffer not hereafter innocent bloode to be cast away, seeing it is no small matter.*' Then a Minister with an admirative replie said to the people that in these wordes he shewed himselfe a traitor, 'because (quoth he) this man saith that if the Queene touch the annoynted of the Pope, she sheddeth innocente bloude.' *M. Paine* turning unto him said, 'Truly you deale very uncharitably with me. For, saith he, I desired my lorde to speak unto her Maiestie, that she suffer not innocent bloode to be caste away,' and then uttered his great affection to the Queene. In course of talke, my *L. Rich* said: '*Paine*, have you not alwaies desire to spende your life for the Queene's death?' *M. Paine* then was in contemplation, and not hearing, answered not. If perchance he had answered affirmatively (not thinking of the word *death*, put so sophistically in the last place, but of *health*) then God (to whom all men's intentions lie open) knoweth what the adversarie would have gathered thereof.

A Minister said that although he denied this treason, yet for all that he was a traitor, 'For, said he, *Campion* and his company denied their treason, and yet it was by more then twoe witnesses proved unto them.' *M. Paine* answered that immediately before their execution he demaunded of them if these accusations of treasons had any grounde? They said by their faith that it was never imagined, nor hard of by them. Then the Minister said *M. Harte* had confessed it, he answered that he would defende no man's doings but his owne, and that he knewe not thereof.

Straight waies they affirmed that he confessed such treason to the *Lady Poole*. He said that he knewe her not. Then

---

The Good Lord give her & her counsel his grace to consider of the matter

These Ministers truely are mad fellowes

A pretie conceit to entrap the innocent man? they sport themselves with innocent mens bloud

The Ministers spoke

There was nothing proved but that there were false witnesses

The divel is a lier & the author of thes lies that his ministers utter

the Minister inferred that his brother confessed to him in his chamber seven years agoe that he talked of such an intention. To this he answered, being somewhat moved, '*Bone Deus!* My brother is, and always hath been a very earnest Protestant, whom yet I know will not say so falsely of me.' And then desired that his brother should be sent for. They called for him, but then he was in the towne. When a sort[24] of us came from the execution we found his brother in our Inne, of whom we asked if this was true, uttering unto him all the matter. He sware unto us with great admiration that it was most false, and tolde us that he would so certify my *L. Rich*; immediately he was sent for to my lorde, and I tooke horse to ride away, and thereof as yet here no more.

See Note 24

To conclude they would not tarry so longe till his brother should be sent for. *M. Paine* often confessed that he died a Christian Catholike priest. They desired *M. Paine* to pray with them in English, but he was attentive to his ende in contemplation, and being often called on by the Ministers to joyne with them in the Lord's Praier, he said that he had praied in a tongue which he well understood. And againe when he was praying, repeating their former requestes, one answered that he then praied in English, perhapps to satisfie the people, for he hard not a worde.

If heretics had any religion they would never desire to pray with one of another faith

After *M. Paine* told them that he said our Lorde's Praier three times and told them that he would say the Psalme *Miserere*, and said it forth. The Minister asked him whether he repented not that he had said Masse, but he heard him not, being in contemplation. After all, very mekely when the ladder was about to be turned he said, '*Jesus, Jesus, Jesus,*' and so did hange not moving hand or foote. They very courtesly caused men to hange on his

A wise question

feete, and set the knot to his eare, and suffered him to hange to death, commaunding *Bull*, the hangman of Newgate, to dispatch, lest he should, as they said, revive, and rebuked him that he did not dispatch speedily. All the towne loved him exceedingly, the keepers and most of the magistrats of the shere. No man seemed in countenance to mislike with him, but much sorowed and lamented his death, who most constantly, Catholikely, patiently and meekely ended this mortal life, to rise triumphantly, his innocency knowen to all the world.

He had been long in prison very ill used, cruelly handeled, and extremely racked. He was once or twise demaunded whether he would goe to their church (for that would have made amendes for all these treasons). 'Why? said he, you say I am in for treason, discharge me of that, and then you shall know further of my minde for the other.' All faier meanes, all foule meanes, all extremitie, all pollicie, were used to finde that which was not. After his racking the Lieutenant sent to him for his farther examining, or rather tormenting, his servant with this letter following:

'I have herewith, sent you pen, inke and paper: and I pray you writte what you have said to *Eliot* and to your *Host* in London, concerning the Queene and the state, and thereof faile not, as you will answer at your peril.'

M. Paine's answer

RIGHT worshipfull, my deutie remembred. Being not able to writte without better handes, I have by your appointment used the helpe of your servant, for answere unto your interrogatories. I have already said sufficient for a man that regardeth his owne salvation, and that, with such advised asseverations uttered, as amongest christian men ought to be beleeved, yet once againe briefly for obedience sake.

First, touching her Maiestie, I pray God long to preserve her highness to his honour and her hartes desire, unto whom I alwaies have and during life will wishe no worse, then to my owne soule. If her pleasure be not that I shall live and serve her as my sovereigne Prince, then will I willingly die her faithful subject, and I trust God's true servant.

Touching the state, I protest, that I am and ever have been free from the knowledge of any practise whatsoever, either within or without the realme, intended against the same; for the verity whereof, as I have often before you and the rest of her grace's commissioners called God to witnes, so doe I now againe, and one day before his Maiestie the truth now not credited will be then revealed.

For *Eliot* I forgive his monstrous wickednes and defie his malicious inventions, wishing that his former behaviour towards others being well knowen, as hereafter it will, were not a sufficient disprofe of these devised sclaunders.

For *host* or other person living in London or els where (unles they be by subornation of my blouddy ennemy corrupted) I know they can, neither for worde, deede, or any disloyaultie iustly touch me, and so before the seat of God, as also before the sight of men, will I answer at my uttermost peril.

Her Maiestie's faithful subiect and your worship's humble prisoner

JOHN PAINE Priest.

*The Arraignement and Martyrdom of M.
Everard Haunse, Priest: who was arraigned
the xxviij Day of Julie* 1581 *and Martyred the xxxj of the same
Moneth*

Chap. XI

M. EVERARD HAUNSE sometime a Minister of the Heretical service, and well beneficed, fell, by God's providence and mercie towards him, into a grevous sicknes, in which as well by that chastisment, as by some special admonitions from above, he beganne to consider of his former life, and the damnable state & function he was in. Whereupon calling for a Catholike Priest, he reconciled himself to the Church, forsooke the sacrilegious function of the Ministrie, abandoned his wrongfully gotten and holden benefice: and so passed over to Remes. Where having lived nere ij yeres in most zelous and studious sort, and by that time through continual exercise well instructed in cases of conscience, and all deuties of Priesthod: he was for the unspeakable desire he had to gain both others, but specially some of his dearest frendes into the unitie of the Church and salvation, much moved to be Priest and to retorne home.

The heretikes say he could not gett lerning inough to be a priest so quickly and yet they thought him lerned inough to be a Minister 4 or 5 yeres before

FATHER EDMUND CAMPION

He had his intent and so came into England. Where he had not been long, but adventuring one day to goe visit certaine prisoners in the Marshalsee, there he was apprehended, & being examined by an officer what he was, and from whence he came, without more adoe confessing boldly himself to be a Catholike, a Priest and a Seminarie man of Rhemes, was thereupon cast into New-gate amongest theeves and laden with yrons. And a few daies after, when the gaile delivery of that prison was holden, he was brought to the barre with other malefactors.

Here *M. Flitwood*, the recorder, sitting in iudgement, asked him where he was made Priest, what was the cause of his comming into England and the like. Which the man of God marvelous resolute without feare or dissimulation told him, affirming the cause of his retorne to be to gaine soules, and that he was made Priest at Rhemes. 'Then, saith he, you are a subject to the Pope?' 'So I am, sir,' saith *M. Haunse*, to which *M. Flitwood* replied, 'Then the Pope hath some superioritie over you?' 'That is true,' quoth he. 'What, in England?' said the Recorder. 'Yea, in England, saith he, for he hath as much authoritie and right in spiritual governement in this realme as ever he had, and as much as he hath in any other countrie, or in Rome itself.' *It is no temporal law that can take from him the right that Christ hath given him*

Upon which most true and syncere confession, the Heretikes (as their fashion is to falsifie all things and by contrived sclaunders to make odious the servants of God) gave out afterward in print that he should say, *That Princes had not any supreamicie or soverantie in their owne realme but the Pope only:* which was far from his and every Catholike man's minde. But upon his former answer, to bring him by course of questions into the compase of some of their new statutes of treason, they asked him further, whether he thought the *How heretikes bely Catholikes*

How, where and when, the Pope is free from error

Pope could not erre? To which though he expressly answered, that in life and maners he might offend, & as in his private doctrine or writing erre also, yet as in iudicial definition and deciding matters of controversie he did never erre. This plaine speach notwithstanding, the ennemies gave out that he should say, *The Pope could not sinne.*

Then they proceded with him further, and demaunded whether the Pope did not iudicially procede in the deposition of the Queene. And thereupon redde a piece of the Bull of *Pius Quintus*, those wordes specially in which he declared her to be an Heretike, and a fautor of Heretikes, and deprived her of all regal authoritie and pretended right of these dominions, absolving all her subiects from her obedience. 'Did he not err, quoth they, in this?' 'I hope,' said *M. Haunse*, he did not.' Which terme, 'I hope,' he used purposely in this matter, and not any other asseveration, because *Pius Quintus* his act was in this case not a matter of doctrine but of fact, wherein he did not affirme that the Pope could not erre. But to goe one step forward, and to bring him into the compasse of the first statut of the last parlement, whereupon they entended streight to endit him. *M. Recorder* asked whether he spake the foresaid thing to persuad other men that heard him, to be of his mind, 'I know not what you meane by persuading, saith he, but I would have all men to believe the Catholike faith as I do.'

That being done and said of each side, order was given to one present, that was learned in the law to drawe an endightement of treason against *M. Haunse*, upon the new statut made in the last parlement, which was out of hand done. The effect whereof was, that the said *Haunse*, being one of the Pope's scollers, and made Priest beyond the seas, was retorned to seduce the Queene's Maiestie's sub-

---

An other forgerie of the Protestants

In a matter of fact the Pope may be misinformed or doe sometimes things that are not profitable for the Church though it be a good mans part to trust that his cheefe pastor doeth al things with some good consideration

Another snare

iects from their obedience, and that he had affirmed the Pope to be his superior here in England, and had as much authoritie in spiritual governement within this realme as ever he had before: saying further, that he hoped *Pius Quintus* erred not in declaring her to be an Heretike, excommunicating and deposing her M. and discharging the subiectes from their othe and obedience towards her, acknowledging that he uttered so much to have others thinke therein as he did, etc.

Which endightement being openly redd, and *M. Haunse* thereon arraigned, he was willed to hold up his hand; he held up his left hand, whereupon the Recorder blamed him, attributing it to some pride or superstition, that being a priest he would not vouchsafe or might not hold up his anointed right hand; but the truth was, he did it for that his right hand was occupied in easing himself by holding up the great boultes wherewith the blessed man was exceedingly laden, for being admonished he forthwith streached forth his right hand.

And being asked if he was guiltie of the thinges conteined in the endightement, after a few wordes, wherein he said that he was not altogether guiltie in those thinges as they were set downe, he yet acknowledged the substance & the sence thereof with great courage and constancie. Whereupon the sentence of death was pronounced against him, in forme well knowen to all men. This done he was retorned to the prison from whence he came: whether Minister *Crowley* and others came to assay his constancie, but after much talke and many persuasions to relent in some point of religion, and to acknowledge his fault towards her Maiestie, when they saw they could not prevaile against the blessed Confessor, they forged to his disgrace and to make him odious, that he should affirme to them in talke, *That treason to the Queene was no sinne before God.* Which sclaunder they were not ashamed to put out in print.

Upon the last of July 1581 he was drawn to Tyborne, where being put into the carte, with cheereful countenance he professed himself to be a Catholike Priest, and most glad to dye for testimonie thereof. And being willed to aske the Queene mercie, and demaunded whether he toke her for his prince and soveraine; he answered that he did take her for his Queene, and that he never offended her Maiestie otherwise then in matters of his conscience, which they have drawn to matters of treason. 'And whereas, saith he, I understand that it hath been geven forth that I should say, *Treason was no offence to God:* I protest, I neither meant nor said any more but that these new made treasons, which are nothing els in deed, but the confession of the Catholike points of religion, were no offences to God, howsoever they were treasons to man.'

Then the Ministers called upon him to pray with them, and to desire the people to assist him. He answered that he might not pray with Heretikes, but desired humbly all Catholikes to pray for him, and with him. And so praying devoutly to himself, the carte was drawn away, and before he was half dead, the rope was cut, and he bowelled alive, and afterward quartered, a spectacle of great edification to the good, and a wonder to every one that looked upon it.

The copie of a letter sent by the said Martyr to his brother

BROTHER, I pray you be careful for my parents, see them instructed in the way of truth, so that you be careful for your own state also. What you shall take in hand that way, thinke no other, but God will send good successe, my praiers shall not be wanting to aide you by God's grace. Give thanks to God for all that he hath sent, cast not yourselfe into dangers wilfully, but pray to God when occasion is offered, you may take it with patience. The comforts of the present instant are unspeakeable, the dignitie too high for a sinner, but God is merciful: Bestowe my things you find ungeven away upon my poore kinsfolkes.

A paire of pantoffls I leave with M. N. for my mother. Twentie shillings, I would have you bestow on them from me, if you can make so much conveniently, some I have lefte with M. N. I owe ten shillings, and two shillings, I pray you see it paied, M. N. will let you understand how, and to whom. Yf you want money to discharge it send to my frendes, you know where, in my name. *Summa Conciliorum* I pray you to restore to M. B., the other bookes you know to whom.

Have me commended to my frends, let them thinke I will not forget them. The day and houre of my birth is at hand, and my Master saith, *Tolle crucem tuam & sequere me.*   *Vale in domino.*

Yours *EVERARD HAUNSE*

Pridie obitus.

The Arraignement and Martyrdom of M. Cuthbert Maine, Priest, and Bachiler of Divinitie: Martyred the 29 *of Novemb.* 1577

Chap. XII

After we had ended the historie of these xii Martyrs, which at the beginning we ment only to writ of, we were desired to add iij others that suffered for the same quarrel these yeres past

The Order of his apprehension

IN the yere 1577 and the moneth of June the superintendent of Execeter being in visitation at a towne called S. Trurie, was requested by the sherife of the sheere and other busie men, that he would aide and assist them to search *M. Tregian's* howse, where *M. Maine* did lye: after some deliberation it was concluded that the sherife, the Bishop's Chauncellor, with divers gentilmen and their servants should take the matter in hand.

As sone as they came to *M. Tregiane's* house the sherife first spake unto him, saying, that he and his company were come to search for one *M. Bourne*, which had committed a fault in London, and so fled into Cornewal, and was in his house, as he was enformed. *M. Tregian* answering that he was not there, and swearing by his faith that he did not know where he was, further telling him, to have his house searched he thought it great discourtesie, for that he was a gentilman as he was, for he did acount his house as his castel: also stoutely denying them, for that they had no commission from the Prince.

The Sherife being very bold, because he had a great company with him, sware by all the othes he could devise, that he would search his howse or else he would kill or be killed, holding his hand upon his dagger as though he would have stabbed it into the gentilman.

This violence being used he had leave to search the howse, the first place they went unto was *M. Maine's* chamber, which being fast shut, they bounsed and beat at the dore. *M. Maine* came & opened it (being before in the garden, where he might have gone from them) as sone as the Sherife came into the chamber, he toke *M. Maine* by the bosome and said unto him, 'What art thou?' and he answered, 'I am a man,' whereat the Sherife being very hot, asked whether he had a coat of maile under his dublet, and so unbuttoned it, and found an Agnus Dei case about his necke, which he toke from him and called him a traitor & rebel with many other opprobrous names.

M. Tregians howse searched

They carried him, his bookes papers and letters, to the superintendent, who when he had talked with him & examined him of his religion, he confessed that he was learned and had gathered very good notes in his bookes, but no favour he shewed him. Thence the sherife carried him from one gentilman's howse to another, until he came to *Lanstone*, where he was cruelly emprisoned, being chained to his bedde posts with a paire of great gives about his legges, and strait commaundement given that no man should repaire unto him.

M. Maine caried to the superintendent

Cruelly imprisoned

Thus he remained in prison from June till Michelmas, at what time the iudges came their circuit, the *Earle of Bedford* was also present at *M. Maine's* arraignment and did deale most in the matter. He was endited for having a Bull, holy graines and an *Agnus Dei*, which was against their

His arraignement

hethenish statutes. *M. Maine* answered negatively to every point of the enditement, and did prove it very well, if they had not been blinded with malice and envie. The Iurie that went upon him were chosen men for the purpose, and thought him worthy of death whether there came any proofs against him or no, because he was a Catholike priest, such is their evangelical conscience. After the twelve had given their verdict *Guiltie*, the Judges gave sentence on him that he should be executed within xv daies, but it was deferred until S. Andrewes day upon what occasion I know not.

The sentence

The Sherife in the meane time went to the court where he was made knight for this notable peece of service, and there he procured a commission that *M. Maine* might be executed, which he sent into the countrey to the Iustices. Three daies befor he was put to death, there came a serving man unto him, and willed him to prepare for death, 'for, saith he, you are to be executed within these three daies at the farthest.' Which gentil admonition *M. Maine* toke very thankefully, and said to the servinge man, that if he had anything to geve, he would rather bestow it upon him, then on any other, for he had done more for him then ever any man did.

He taketh the advertisment of his death thankfully

After that advertisment he gave himself ernestly to praier and contemplation until his death. The second night after he gave himself to these spiritual exercises, there was seen a great light in his chamber, betweene twelve & one of the clocke, in so much that some of the prisoners that lay in the next romes, called unto him to know what it was, for they knew very well that he had neither fire nor candel, he answered, willinge them to quiet themselves, for it did nothing appertaine unto them.

His spiritual exercises

At the day of his execution many Iustices and gentil-

OF FATHER EDMUND CAMPION   107

men came to see him and brought with them two proud ministers, which did dispute with him, whom he did confute in every point. But the Iustices and gentilmen who were blind iudges in their doings would heare nothing of that, but they affirmed that the ignorant Ministers were much better learned then he, albeit they confesse he died very stoutely, whereat they did much marveil, saying to the ignorant people, that he could avouch no scripture for his opinion, which was most untrue. For I know by the report of honest men that were present that he did confirme every point in question with testimonies of scriptures and doctors, and that abundantly. *The Ministers dispute with him*

This ended he was to be drawen a quarter of a mile to the place of execution, and when he was to be laid on the sled, some of the Iustices moved the Sherife's deputie, that he would cause him to have his head laid over the carre, that it might be dashed against the stones in drawing, and *M. Maine* offered himself that it might be so, but the Sherife's deputie would not suffer it. *A barbarous request* *M. Maines humilitie*

When he came to the place of execution he kneled downe and praied. As he was on the ladder, and the rope about his necke, he would have spoken to the people, but the Iustices would not suffer him, but willed him to say his praiers, which he did very devoutely. And as the hangeman was about to turne the ladder, one of the Iustices spake to him in this manner: 'Now villaine and traitor thou knowest that thou shalt dye, and therefore tell us whether *M. Tregian* and *Sir John Arundel* did know of these thinges which thou art condemned for; and also what thou doest know by them.' *A protestants spirit*

M. Maine answered him againe very mildly, saying, 'I do know nothing by *M. Tregian* and *Sir John Arundel*, but that they be good and godly gentilmen, and as for the thinges I am condemned for, they were onely knowen to me and to no others.' Then he was cast of the ladder, saying, *In manus tuas*, etc., and knocking his breast.

No Gentilmans bloud in such cruel harts

Some of the gentilmen would have had him cut downe straightway, that they might have had him quartered alive, but the Sherife's deputie would not, but let him hang till he was dead. After he was quartered, one quarter was sent to S. Probus where he was taken, an other to Wade-brig, the third to Bastabile in Devonsheir where he was borne, the fourth and his head remaine in Lanstone where he was executed.

He was made a Minister

This blessed man, *M. Maine*, borne in Bastable in Devonsheir, had an old schismatical priest to his uncle, and well beneficed, who being very desirous to leave his benefice to this his nephew, brought him up at scholle, and when he was xviij or xix yeres old, got him to be made minister. At what time (as *M. Maine* himself with great sorow and diep sighes did often tell me) he knew neither what ministrie nor religion meant. Being sent after to Oxford, he heard his course of logike in Alborne hall, and there proceeded Bachiler of Art.

His degrees in schole

At that time S. John's Colledge wanted some good fellow to play his part at the communion table, to play which part *M. Maine* was invited and hired. In this colledge and function he lived many yeres, being of so milde a nature, and of such sweet behaviour, that the Protestants did greatly love him, & the Catholikes did greatly pietie him, seeing so honest a nature cast away upon so contemptible a function; in so much that some dealing with him, and advertising him of the damnable state he stoode in, he was easely persuaded their doctrine to be heretical, and withal brought to lament and deplore his owne miserable state and condition.

And so being in harte and minde a persuaded Catholike continued yet in the same colledg for some yeres, and there proceded M. of Art, and every Sunday gave them a drie communion, for as I thinke he never gave them a *wett supper* but once, at what time all the communicants put that prophane bread into their bosomes and did cast it afterward either to dogges or upon the donghill, as *M. Read*, then a hote Protestant and one of these communicants, now a great preacher and my *L. Treasurer's* chaplain, can best tell you. Some of his familiars being already beyond the seas for their conscience did so solicit him by letters to leave that damnable function of the Ministrie and invited him to come to Doway, one of these letters by chaunce fell into the superintendent's hands of London, who dispatched a perseuant straight to Oxford for *M. Maine* and some others. The rest appeared and were sent to prison, but by chaunce *M. Maine* was then in his countrey, and being advertised by his countreiman and frend, *M. Ford* (then Fellow of Trinitie Colledg in Oxford, and of late martyred) that there was processe out for him, he toke shipping on the coast of Cornwal and so went to Doway when the seminary there was but newly erected.

Where falling to divinitie and keeping the privat exercises within the howse diligently, and doing the publike exercises in the scholles with commendation, after some yeres proceded Bachiler of Divinitie and was made priest, and desirous partly to honor God in this sacred order, and to satisfie for that he had dishonored him by taking the sacrilegious title of Ministrie, partly inflamed with zeal to

marginalia:
A drie communion
A weet supper rightly handled
He went to Doway
Made Bachiler of Divinitie

save soules, he returned towards England together with *M. John Paine*, who was since martyred, the 14 of April in the yere 1576. *M. Maine* placed himself in his owne countrey with a Catholike and vertuous gentilman, *M. Tregian*, where he had not been a full yere but he was taken in the order above specified.

When the adversarie made *M. Maine* this proffer to have his life if he would sweare upon a booke that the Queene was supreme head of the Church of England, and if he did refuse, then to be hanged drawen and quartered, he tooke the Bible into his hands, made the signe of the crosse upon it, kissed it and said, *The queene neither ever was, nor is, nor ever shall be the head of the Church of England.*

A most true othe

The Arraignement and Condemnation of M. John Nelson, Priest, who was Martyred the xiij of February the year M.D. lxxviij

Chapter XIII

THIS vertuous Priest, *M. Nelson*, was taken in London upon the first of December in the yere M.D. lxxvij, late in the evening, as he was saying the Nocturne of the Mattins for the next day folowing, and was presently sent to prison upon suspition of Papistry, as they terme the Catholike faith.

And after v or vj daies he was brought furth to be examined before the high commissioners, and there they tendered the othe of the Queene's supremacie unto him, the which he refused to take. Being asked why he would not sweare, he answered because he never had heard or read that any laye Prince could have that preeminence. Being farther demaunded, who then was the head of the Church, he answered sincerely and boldly, *That the Pope's Holines was*, to whom that supreme authoritie was due, as being *Christ's vicar and the lawful successor of S. Peter.*

Secondly they asked him his opinion of the religion now practized in England, to which he answered promptly that

His apprehension

He is examined of his faith

He refuseth the othe of the supremacie

He maketh a true confession

THE DEATH & MARTYRDOM

The English religion is schismatical and heretical

it was both schismatical and heretical. Whereupon they bid him define what schisme was, he told them that it was, *A voluntary departure from the unitie of the Catholike Roman faith.*

They seek to entrappe him

Then they inferred, 'What, is the Queene a schismatike, or no?' He answered, he could not tell, because he knew not her minde in setting furth or manteyning of the religion now publikly used in England. The commissioners replied, that the Queene did promulgat it and manteine it; and urging him that if she so did, then whether she were a schismatike and heretike or no?

M. *Nelson* pawsed a while, as being looth to exasperat his prince, if he might have chosen [otherwise], but yet more loth to offend God and his owne conscience or to give scandal to the world, answered conditionally after this sort: '*If she be the setter furth* (quoth he) *and defender of this religion now practized in England, then she is a Schismatike and an Heretike.*' Which answer when they had wronge from him, they said he had spoken inough, they sought for no more at his handes.

They drive men into the compase of treason of purpose

His arraignement

And so he was desmissed and sent backe to prison. And about vii weekes after he was brought furth to his arraignement, and the same interrogatories propunded againe, and he answering still the selfe same to every question, as he had donne before, sentence of death was pronounced against him, as against one guiltie of treason, the first day of February, the yere 1578.

His constancie of minde

When the sentence was pronounced against him, he never changed his countenance, nor there never appeared in him any signe of a troubled minde, but toke his condemnation very meekly, and prepared himself with a good courage for death. The gailour's wife, moved with compassion, offered him wine, thereby as she thought to aswage the hevines of his minde. But he would not tast it, saying he rather desired a cup of cold water, as more meet for him. And from the houre the sentence was prononced against him till the houre of his death, he tooke no other foode but bread and small beere.

He did voluntary penance after his condemnation

He was so delited with praier and secret meditation that he would not heare of any other things willingly, especially if they were worldly matters. In so much that when a frend of his (for his greater comfort and the more to animate him against the terrors of death) wished him to read and meditat upon the lives and deaths of martyrs, as they are set downe in the service according to the use of Rome, albeit he misliked not of the counsel, answered yet, that he had enough to occupie his minde withal, and to meditat upon full well.

His minde only upon heavenly things

He was ful of spiritual comforts

And being put in minde by the same frend, with what alacritie and ioye of minde many thousande martyrs had suffered exquisite tormentes for Christ's sake, and that they never complained or shrunke thereat, he answered, that that cogitation came ofte to his minde and that he tooke such comfort thereof, that he doubted nothing but that he should finde and feele the grace of God's consolation in the middest of his agonie.

What things he specially tok comfort

And surely this resolutnes of minde, and willingnes to dye, came of this, that the Thursday before his arraignment and death he had clensed his conscience by confession, and had fortified himself by receiving the B. Sacrament of the Altar. For a priest comming to visit him, with others in his companie, desirous to communicat at *M. Nelson's* hands, wishing it might be upon *Candlemas day* because of the solemnitie of the feast. But after they had

The cheefe causes of his comforts

considered on the matter a while they saw it was no fit day, because such festival daies are more subiect to suspition then other daies are, and therefore they concluded to difer it till the day after *Candlemas day.* But *M. Nelson* wished rather to prevent the feast and to communicat upon the Thursday before, which was done. Though that neither he himself, nor any of his frends, had any the least coniecture that he should so shortly come to his Martyrdome. And behold the very next day after, word was brought him that on the morrow he should be arraigned, and undoutedly condemned, if he did not revoke his former wordes, and so it fell out in deed as you have hard.

Upon Munday the iij of February being the day of his Martyrdom, he came, very early before day, up to the higher part of the prison: whereas from Saterday till then he had been kept in a low dongeon. Two of his neerest kinsmen comming unto him, found him ernest at his praiers with his hands ioyned together and lifted up, in so much that the other prisoners there present did both marke it and wounder at it much.

When they had talked a while together, & he seeing them so full of sorrow that they had much ado to abstaine from weeping, yet for all that was nothing moved himself, neither gave any signe or apparance of sorowe either in voice or countenance, but rebuked them, saying that he looked for some comfort and consolation of them in that case, and not by their teares be occasioned to greefe and sorow of minde. Willing them farther to lament and weepe for their owne sinnes and not for him, for he had a sure confidence that all should goe well with him.

When his kinsmen tooke their last farewell of him, they

It was Gods special providence that he should so resolve

His demeanor the day of his death

His cheerefulnes in God

fell into such immoderat teares and lamentations that he was somewhat moved therewith, but staied and repressed nature by and by, and so dismissed them. And they were no sooner gone but two proud ministers of Satan came unto him, seeking by all means to remove him from his faith, but in vaine, for he utterly refused to have any talke with them, wiling them to let him be in quiet, and so they did, and departed from him. *The Divels Ministers had no power o'ver him*

When he was brought furth of the prison, and to be laide on the herdle, some of the officers exhorted him to aske the Queene's Maiestie, whom he had highly offended, forgeveness, he answered, '*I will aske her no pardon, for because I never offended her.*' At which wordes the people that stode about him raged, and threatened him that if he would not he should be hanged like a traitor as he was, '*Well*, saith he, *God's will be done. I perceive that I must die, and suerly I am redy to die with a good will. For better it is to abide all punishment, be it never so grevous here, then to suffer the eternal torments of hell fire.*' *His innocencie*

His willingnes to dye

Being come to the place of execution, and put into the carte, the first wordes he spoke were, *In manus tuas, domine, etc.* Then he besought such of the standers by as were Catholikes to pray with him and for him, saying either in Latin or English the *Pater noster*, the *Ave Maria*, and the *Creede*, which he himself said in Latine, adding therto the *Confiteor*, and the Psalmes *Miserere* & *De profundis*, which finished turning himself round about to all the people, said unto them in this sort, 'I call you all this day to witnes that I dye in the unitie of the Catholike Church, and for that unitie do now most willingly suffer my bloude to be shed. And therefor I beseech God, and request you all to pray for the same, that it would please God of his great *His praiers at his death*

A notable profession & his praier

mercie to make you, and all others that are not, trewe Catholique men and both to live and die in the unitie of our holy mother the Catholike Roman Church.'

The deceived peoples clamor

At which words the people cried out, 'Hence! Away with thee and thy Catholike Romish faith.' But this, notwithstanding he repeated the same praier againe. Then he requested to be forgeven of all men as well absent as present, if he had offended any, protesting that he forgave all his enemies and persecutors, desiring God also to forgeve them. Here againe he was willed to aske the Queene's forgeveness, the which he refused to do for a while, at the last he said, 'If I have offended her or any els, I aske her and all the world forgevenes, as I forgeve all.'

He praieth for his persecutors

His last praier

And so the hangman being willed to dispatch, M. Nelson praied a little while to himself, and then requested such of the assembly as were Catholikes to pray with him, *That Christ by the merites of his bitter Passion would receive his soule into everlasting ioye.* When the carte was drawen away, a great number cried out with loude voice, *Lord, receive his soule.*

He was cruelly executed

He was cut downe before he was halfe dead, dismembered and ripped up, and as the hangman plucked out his hart, he lifted himself up a little, and as some that stode nere report, spake these wordes, *I forgive the Queene and all that were causers of my death.* But I, though I saw his lipps move, yet heard not so much: and the hangman had iij or iiij blowes at his head, before he could strike it of. His quarters were hanged on four gates of the citie, and his head set upon London Bridge: and thus he changed this mortal life with immortalitie. God be blessed for him; and blessed be the memorie of this his Martyrdom amongest men in all our posterities. Amen.

This man from his youth had the zele of God & of his house, excedingly detesting, ever sith he had the knowledg of the truth specially since he was made Priest and instructed beyond the seas, the first great necligence that most men of our Countrey, even Catholikes, in the beginning of this Queene's raigne committed, in goeing to the Communion, Church and service of heretikes; much glorifying God, that he vouchsafed afterwards to open that error to the people, and to geve to so many the grace of reconciliation and constancie to resist that wickednes: and to follow the example of their cheefe pastors therein, the holy Bishops and Confessors, that then were deprived and in prison for the same.

After his death it is credibly reported, that some sicke persons were restored miraculously to health by his holy Relikes. And a man worthy of all credit, riding downe from London northward straight upon his execution, spake these wordes to a grave person that told me the storie. 'It is now come to passe (said he) that *John Nelson* foretold me vij yeres since *That he should die for the Catholike faith.*' And divers others may well remember how he would often times say: 'That the Catholike religion would never be restored in England until many should shedd their bloud for confession and testimonie of the same.'

Which we may undoubtedly take, both for a prophecie of this great persecution, and also for the conversion of our country through the acceptable cry of so much holy innocent bloud, so meekely yelded on the one side, and so uniustly spilled on the other. Which God graunt for his Sonne's sake, the Head and rewarder of all these blessed Martyrs.

— Note this point wel

— He foretold his owne death and this persecution

The Martyrdom of Thomas Sherwod
1578 *the vij of February*

Chap. XIV

THIS was a lay man, and yong of yeres, but by the special grace of God, and his father's, a holy confessor's, example and instruction, especially geven to the Catholike faith, pietie and great penance. He was apprehended in the streats of London ready to goe over to the seminarie at Remes by the wickednes of *Martine Tregonian* [Tregonwell]. He by ill company and education became a Calvinist, and upon suspicion that this yong man brought Priests to say Masse in his mother's house, who was a good Catholike lady, meeting him by chaunce in London cried, 'A traitor, a traitor! Stay, Stay the traitor!'

Whereupon the people durst do no lesse, but ishew out of their shopps and apprehend him; so they brought him to the *Recorder*, his accuser having nothing in the world to charge him withal; but because it was for suspicion of religion, they quickly entrapped him by enterrogatories of *Pius Quintus*' Bull, of the excommunication of the Queene's religion, and whether she was an heretike, and of her spiritual soveraignitie, unto all which he answered like a true Christian man both then and afterward at his arraignement. After about vj monethes miraculous constancie, suffering of most cruel dongeons, yrons, famine & racking almost to death (being the first that was racked for mere matter of faith in our memories), at length, the day and yere above specified, he was drawen to Tyborne, hanged, cut downe, boweled alive, and so devided and his head and quarters set up, he gloriously toke his leave of this world, and is received into the eternal tabernacles in glorie and felicitie eternal.

Gentil Reader, consider our difficulties in
printing, & beare with the
faults escaped us.

FINIS

A NOTE ON THE ILLUSTRATIONS

THE six engravings, which are here reproduced, were published from copper plates in the first edition of the Italian translation of this book, printed at Macerata in 1583. I have not found them in any subsequent editions. They represent to us the usual course of the persecution, rather than the history of any particular martyr, though Campion is mentioned once. We are shown how the Catholics were arrested, mocked, led off to prison, examined, tortured, drawn and executed.

It is quite possible that these plates were originally engraved for Father Persons's well-written and popular Latin tract, entitled *De Persecutione Anglicana*, which made a great impression abroad, and which treated of the sufferings of the English Catholics in this general way.

The connexion of the plates with the *De Persecutione* may further be argued from the striking incident of the flogging at the cart's tail, and the branding of John Typet (also written Typper), in plate 3. This brave youth, after his courageous confession, became a Carthusian monk, and rose to high office in that Order. Allen, however, does not allude to him at all. So the inspiration must have come from elsewhere.

These pictures give the earliest representations of the sufferings of the English martyrs, and as Allen's book was the seed, as it were, of the subsequent martyrologies, so these pictures afforded ideas to various subsequent artists. The first and chief of these was Niccolo Circiniani (the eldest of three painters who have called themselves Dalle Pomerancie), who was employed in 1583-1584 in painting frescoes of the martyrdoms in the church of the English Martyrs at Rome, which frescoes were engraved by Giovanni Battista Cavalieri and published under the title, *Ecclesiæ Anglicanæ Trophæa*, Rome, 1584. The plates regarding the English Martyrs were reprinted by Father John Morris.

Circiniani has evidently based his plates 31, 32, 33 (Morris, plates 5, 6, 7) on our plates 4, 5, 6; while his 34 (Morris, 8) draws from both 2 and 3 of our series. Whilst our plates give us realistically the costume of the day,

Circiniani has represented all but the martyrs in classical attire (or in classical absence of attire). Except that he corrects the gallows into the "triple tree" of Tyburn (probably the earliest representation of it known), his treatment is really inferior to that of our plates.

Richard Verstegan, in his *Theatrum Crudelitatis Hæreticorum nostri temporis*, Antwerp, 1592, in his plates on pp. 71, 73, 79, has used our plates 2, 4, 3; while his p. 83 takes in our 5 and 6. He has also borrowed from Circiniani.

The frontispiece is taken from a very rare plate at the British Museum (P. II, c. iv, 2 sub.) The inscription is in Latin.

Father Persons, in the unfinished *Life and Martyrdom of Father Edmund Campion*, c. xiv, thus described him, when he came to Rome from Germany, "And surely I remember he came after so venerable a manner as might move devotion. For he came in grave priests [gown] with long [beard and] hair, after the fashion of Germany." It is in this dress that Campion is represented here. The exceedingly high collar of the German habit has the effect of making the neck look abnormally short. When this is allowed for, the portrait, though of course not drawn from nature, corresponds fairly with the sub-contemporary portrait formerly at the Gesù (*Lives of the English Martyrs*, ii, 357).

The print is German sixteenth century. A copy of Bromley's *Catalogue of British Portraits* has this note on it, "£8 8s. 0d.: Extremely rare. I never saw another copy."

I. *APPREHENSION*

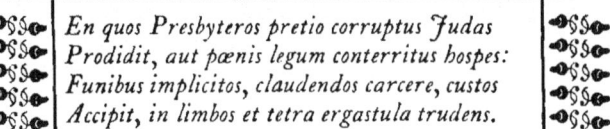

En quos Presbyteros pretio corruptus Judas
Prodidit, aut pœnis legum conterritus hospes:
Funibus implicitos, claudendos carcere, custos
Accipit, in limbos et tetra ergastula trudens.

A SPY or False Brother will sometimes cry upon the Martyr in the street, as Tregonwell did on Sherwood. The Rabble, armed with the first weapons to hand, runs out upon him, and even the boys throw stones.

At last, surrounded by pike-men, tied with a rope, mocked by onlookers, he is led to prison, where the Keeper has ready the dungeon and the gyves.

II. *THE ROAD TO PRISON*

Captos dum celebrant, in sacro lictor amictu
Raptat per medias populo insultante plateas.
Capti rure alii, manibus pedibusque ligati
Imponuntur equis, primasque vehuntur ad urbes.

IF the Priest be captured at Mass, or with his Vestments, he is led to gaol clothed in them. Even the ladies may be dragged along with him.

F. Campion was carried to the Tower, pinioned and his feet tied beneath the horse's belly, an inscription on his hat, Torchmen in front and the Sheriff behind. The Keeper received him with mock solemnity.

III. *EXAMINATION WITH TORMENT*

Devincti ad carros, perque urbis compita ducti,
Libera servili lacerantur terga flagello.
Supplicio hoc functis, mox tanquam erronibus aures
Perfossæ, igniti terebrantur acumine ferri.

SOME Catholics are flogged at the Cart's tail. Some are branded with irons, which are heated close by. But examination to find matter of death against oneself and others is worse still, and the Ministers are ever near to dispute.

IV. *THE RACK*

Ut quibus excepti domibus mysteria Christi
Egerunt, quosque a funesto schismate sanctæ
Junxere Ecclesiæ prodant, et talia multa,
Distendunt miseros diris cruciatibus artus.

THOSE who resist the lesser torments are racked. Their hands and feet are extended by ropes and windlasses while the questioning continues. Other prisoners are kept near enough to hear the cries and moans of the sufferer, and are warned to avoid his fate.

V. TO TYBURNE

In crate viminea positi, lorisque ligati,
Per saxa ad furcas et per loca fœda trahuntur.
Carnifices laqueos, cultrosque, ignesque parati
Expediunt, primæque attendunt tempora mortis.

PINIONED to the wicker hurdle, which is dragged by a sorry nag, the Martyr is drawn from the Tower to Tyburne. Ministers worry him with arguments and quotations, but he turns away. In the distance the fire is crackling. One executioner prepares the noose, while another sharpens the knife. The cart is waiting.

VI. *EXECUTION*

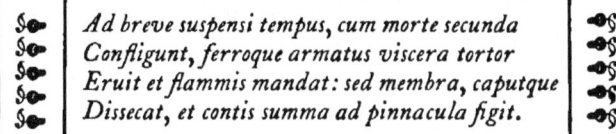

*Ad breve suspensi tempus, cum morte secunda
Confligunt, ferroque armatus viscera tortor
Eruit et flammis mandat: sed membra, caputque
Dissecat, et contis summa ad pinnacula figit.*

CUT down ere fully dead, the Martyr sits up after the fall. The executioner cuts out his heart, which is shown to the people, then cast into the fire. The body is quartered, and the head and quarters are carried back on poles to be set over the city gates.

THE NOTES

1, p. 2. *All to bemoyled*, i.e. altogether covered with mire, cf. Murray's *New English Dictionary on Historical Principles*, Oxford, 1888, under *All*, c. 15, and *Bemoil*.

2, p. 2. The whole of this speech, except for paragraph 3 and the comments added in brackets, is taken verbatim from Vallenger's *True Report* . . . . *observed and written by a Catholike priest, which was present thereat*, including the use of the *first* person, 'I learnt,' 'I noted,' in paragraphs 8 and 10. See 'I myself,' p. 8, 'I add,' p. 48.

3, p. 3. *I must graunt unto you*. The Italian translation has *bisogna ch' io mi vi renda*. See Murray under *Grant*, 7 (2).

4, p. 4. *Quid pro quo like il poticario*. According to ancient druggists each drug had its *succedaneum* or substitute, 'next best thing' or '*quid pro quo*.' See C. A. M. Fennell, *The Stanford Dictionary of Anglicised Words and Phrases*.
Il poticario, printed *il poticaries*. The Italian translation gives, '*a guisa di spetiali trascurati*,' 'like careless druggists.' See also Murray, *Apothecary*.

5, p. 4. The full title of the *Advertisement* was *An advertisement and Defence of Truth against her backbiters, and specially against the whispering favourers and colourers of Campion's and the rest of his confederate's treasons*. 4to. C. Baker, 1581.

6, p. 5. The book alluded to was Munday's *Discoverie of Edmund Campion and his confederates, . . . whereunto is added the execution of Edmund Campion, Ralph Sherwin, and Alexander Briant*, Published by A.M., 1582, Black Letter, copy in British Museum; reprinted in Holinshed. Of this book Hallam says that it was written with 'a savageness and a bigotry which, I am sure, no scribe of the Inquisition could have surpassed.'

7, p. 21. In the original the Latin text is given, because the martyr 'had a special grace in that language,' but it is here omitted, as it may be found in all collections of Campion's Latin Writings.

8, p. 26. There is a sub-contemporary manuscript copy of these verses in the Bodleian Library, from which they have been reprinted by Dr Jessopp. *One Generation of a Norfolk House*, 1878, pp. 97–102, with notes, p. 96. The title there is *An Epitaphe of the lyfe and deathe of the most famouse clerke and vertuouse priest, Edmund Campion, and reverend father of the meeke societie of the blessed name of Jesus*. The variant readings are, upon the whole, slightly inferior to those of the printed version. The poem had been handed about in manuscript copies and had lost a little of its accuracy in transcription. The chief variants are: *verse* 5, *line* 6, *for* erring, hearing; v. 17, l. 6, *for* toys, ioys, *and for* blaspheme not in thy vain (vein), blaspheme not thou in vain; v. 18, l. 3, *for* reuest (revest), rest; v. 20, l. 6, *for* inward, watered; v. 26, l. 2, *for* Is't, lest, *and for* us, our.

9, p. 29. *Elderton, William*, the ballad writer, see *Dictionary of National Biography*, xvii, 173. The verses here alluded to appeared at the end of Munday's *Discoverie of Edmund Campion* already mentioned, and have been reprinted by Mr J. P. Collier. *John a Kent and John a Cumber*, with other tracts by A. Munday, Shakespeare Society, 1851.

10, p. 36. The names are supplied from the Italian and Latin versions.

11, p. 40. The indictments here threatened were actually brought into court, and found to be 'true bills,' on June 28, 1581. The list of the persons indicted is now much damaged, but the names of 'Ralphe Sheringe clerk, Thomas Cotham clerk, and Robert Johnson clerk, all of the parish of the church of St Peter-ad-vincula within the Tower of London,' are still legible. J. Cordy Jeaffreson, *Middlesex County Records*, 1886, I, 124.

12, p. 41. The phrase is obscure. The Italian has, 'Stracco per gl' essercitij spirituali,' the Latin, 'Licet bene agendo defatigatus fortasse vobis videri possem.'

13. p. 42. *Corrasies*, corrosives. *Italian*, 'cordogli'; *Latin*, 'magnas rerum asperitates.' This word is given in Murray's Dictionary under 'Corsie.'

14, p. 49. *A pottle pot. Ital.* un pocale, *Lat.* fere duo sextarii (i.e. three pints). A pottle-pot is a large tankard, the precise measure of which is said to have been two quarts.

15, p. 50. *Swoond*. In original 'sounded,' a Middle-English variant.

16, p. 50. *Bobb*—to pomel, or strike.

17, p. 51. A Latin translation of the whole letter will be found in the *Concertatio*, and an English retranslation in Foley, *Records*, IV, 355. Allen had altogether omitted the lengthy prologue; but, as this somewhat obscures the sense, I have made up from it an opening sentence, which will, I think, make the martyr's meaning clear.

18, p. 58. Allen's marginal note shows that the sense is 'Fourteen years before 1582 the deposition of Princes was discussed at Oxford, and approved, though it was not determined who should carry out the deposition.' This must refer to the year 1568, when the deposition of Queen Mary Stuart by her subjects was frequently debated.

19, p. 62. This prayer, said to be by St Augustine, was usually included in the *Horæ B.V. ad usum Sarum*, E. Hoskins, *Horæ B.V.M.*, 1901, p. 123.

20, p. 72. This report of the Martyr's conference with Munday should be compared with Munday's own account of it in his *Breefe and true reporte of the Execution of certaine tray-tours*, 1582, reprinted by Dom Norbert Birt in *The Downside Review*, Dec. 18, 1891, pp. 215-236. Munday of course represents himself as victorious.

21, p. 85. This was really Humphrey Ely, LL.D., formerly president of St John's, Oxford. He afterwards returned to Rheims, and was doubtless Allen's authority for the episode here related. See *D. N. B.* xvii, 344: Gillow, ii, 164: Camm, ii, 543.

22, p. 90. 'Privy Coat,' i.e., a light coat of mail that could be concealed under other clothes. 'Dagges,' i.e., pistols.

23, p. 91. The Latin translation turns *L. Peter* into Dominæ Peters, viduæ Guilhelmi Peters. The Italian translates the last sentence, 'venne . . . con una sicurtà, persu-adendolo d'andar seco . . . accio fosse presente al suo contratto matrimoniale.

24, p. 95. *A sort*, i.e. a company. (*Ital.* alcuni.)

25, p. 102. The 'Sclaunder put out in print' against Hanse is discussed by Dom Bede Camm, *Lives of English Martyrs*, ii, 64.

THE INDEX

Abingdon, 11
Allen, William, Card., 7, 90, 91; *Intro.* vij
Allen, Mayor of Dover, 22, 84, 85, 86
Allen, Gabriel, 22
Andrewes, Mr, 86, 87
Arundell, Sir John, 107
Avignon, 64

Barnstaple, 108
Bosgrave, James, S.J., 39, 74
Bourne, Mr, 104
Briant, Alexander, S.J., M., 2, 3, 7, 9, 20, 47-56
Bristow, Dr Richard, 63, 73, 80, 90, 91

Campion, Edmund, S.J., M., 1-33, 94; sister of, 20
Charke, William, preacher, 42, 68, 70
Cobham, Henry Brooke, Ld. 85-87
Collington *vere* Colleton, John, 10
Colnbrook, 12
Cottam, Thomas, S.J., 67, 74, 77, 78, 79, 80-2, 88
Coudridg, —, 72
Crowley [?Robert], minister, 72, 101

Douay, 6, 36, 109
Dover, 8, 10, 22, 84-86
Dudley, R., Earl of Leicester, 5, 36, 76, 90

Egerton, Sir Thomas, Solicitor-General, 63
Elderton, William, 29
Elliot, George, 10, 11, 28, 89-93, 96, 97
Elizabeth, Queen; *Intro.* xvij
Emerson, " Little Ralph," S.J., 22
England, Bishop for, 37
Exeter, 104

Field, a preacher, 78
Filby, W., M., 11, 67-70, 76
Fleetwood, William, Recorder of London, 99, 118
Ford, Thomas M., 10, 57-62, 109

Gaudy, Judge, 92
Goldwell, Thomas, Bp of St Asaph, 37, 38
Gregory XIII, 68

Hammond, Dr John, 40, 58, 63
Hart, John, 39, 76, 84, 94
Hatton, Sir Christopher, 91
Haunse, Everard, M., 98-103; his mother, 103; brother, 103

Havard (*vere* Humphrey Ely), 85, 86, 87
Henley, 11
Henry VIII, 65
Hopton, Lady, 89
Hopton, Sir Owen, 12, 14, 20, 21, 40, 49, 50, 89
Howard, Lord Charles, 5, 35

India, 55
Ireland, 6, 47, 69

Johnson, *alias* Laurence Richardson, M., 3, 4, 67, 74-76, 77-83
Johnson, Robert, M., 57, 62-66

Kirby, Luke, M., 67-74, 77, 78
Knollys, Sir Francis, 2, 3, 35

Launceston, 105, 108
Lea, Lye William, a barrister, 18, 29
Lewes [?David], 58, 63
Lidcote, Mr, 11
London, Places in: Cheapside, 87, cross in, 12; Counter, 48; Fish Street, 79, 86, 87; Holborn, 68; Inner Temple, 18; London Bridge, 116; Marshalsea, 39, 88, 99; Newgate, 96; St Andrew's, Holborn, 68; Star Inn, 86, 87; Tower of, 1, 3, 12, 14, 16, 27, 30, 39, 41, 48-50, 57, 67, 71, 88, Coldharbour in, 20, Lieutenants' Hall in, 40, Walesboure dungeon, in, 50; Tyburn, 1, 20, 30, 57, 67, 88, 102, 119; Westminster Hall, 50, 88.
Lyford, 10

Maine, Cuthbert M., 104-110, uncle of, 108
Martyrdoms, incidents of, *Intro.*, xij-xviij
Mary, Queen of Scotland, 90
Maximilian, Emperor, 7
Markham, Sir John, Judge, 18
Martin, Sir Richard, Sheriff, 57, 58, 60, 69, 73, 74
Mary Tudor, Queen, 64, 73
Moore, Mr, Q.C., 90, 92
Morice, Mr, 90
Munday, Anthony, 5, 28, 58, 60, 63, 64, 70, 71, 75, 77

Nelson, John, M., 111-119
Nichols, John, 71, 75
Nonesuch, 88
Norton, Thomas, 20, 28, 48-50

Oatlands, 88
Orton, Henry, 84
Oxford, 1, 5, 11, 47, 58, 77, 108, 109; Alban Hall, 108; St John Baptist College, 1, 5, 108; Trinity College, 109

Payne, John, M., 89-97, 110; his brother, 95
Persons, Robert, S.J., 22, 39, 49
Petre, Lady, 91
Pius V, Pope, *Intro.*, xvj
Poole, Lady, 94
Popham, Sir John, 19, 63
Pound, Thomas, lay brother, S.J., 3

Read, Mr, 109
Reynolds, John, 77

Rheims, 7, 36–38, 47, 57, 60, 63, 71, 84, 98, 99, 118
Rich, Robert, Lord, 93, 94, 95
Richardson, Laurence, M., 3, 4, 36, 67, 74, 76, 77–83
Rishton, Edward, 36, 84
Robinson, —, 70
Robsart, Amy, Lady Dudley, 5
Rome, 6, 7, 36, 47, 57, 60, 70, 76
Roscarrock, Nicholas, 39, 40
Rouen, 37, 42
Russell, Francis, Earl of Bedford, 105

St Andrew's, Minister of, 80
St Omers, 21
St Probus, 108
Saunders, or Sander, Nicholas, 47, 63, 69, 73, 80
Shert, John, M., 57–62
Sherwin, Ralph, M., 1, 18, 20, 34-46, 55, 57
Sherwood, Thomas, M., 118, 119

Sledd, 28, 75, 83, 84
Sone, Dr, 92
Stevens, a searcher, 84
Story, Dr John, M., 21

Tempest, William, 90, 91
Topcliffe, Richard, 68, 71, 73, 80, 81
Tregian, Mr Francis, 104, 107, 110
Tregonwell, Martin, 118; mother of, 118
Truro, 104

Wadebridge, 108
Walsingham, Sir Francis, 76, 90
Westmorland, Charles Neville, Earl of, 90
White, Sir Thomas, 5
Withers, Dr, 92
Woodstock, 36
Woodward, John, 42, 43

Yates, Mr, 10

Printed in Great Britain
by Amazon